A Country Glipe

JIMMY RAFFERTY

Copyright © 2013 Jimmy Rafferty

All rights reserved.

ISBN:1492898384
ISBN-13:9781492898382

DEDICATION

This book is dedicated to my wife and kids, who have had to listen to this rubbish for years.

CONTENTS

	Acknowledgments	i
1	Born and bred – and buttered?	1
2	The place	11
3	Being a we'an	20
4	Visitors	43
5	Being a gosoon	55
6	Farming	61
7	Being a cub	68
8	Towards civilization	81
9	Poems	85
10	Poems : The winners!	134
	About the Author	155

ACKNOWLEDGMENTS

A huge thanks to the 'Bard of Armagh' humorous verse contest, without which none of this would have happened.

It is a unique event – a great audience and a great atmosphere, where everyone is made welcome, and encouraged. I used to have a bad stammer when I was at school, (and for many years afterwards) and if anyone had told me that I would voluntarily get up in front of a thousand people to speak, I'd have called them mad.

Thanks to the 'Bard' for all the fun I have had since!

1 BORN AND BRED – AND BUTTERED?

I am reliably informed that I was born at a very early age, and began to grow up almost immediately.

I cannot comment with any certainty on this, as my memory of the event is rather sketchy to say the least, so I only have my mother's word for it. Mind you, her memory of it was well maintained, as it was not an easy birth, and she was inclined to recount the full horrors of it to other mothers at the drop of a hat. Usually with me sitting there, writhing with embarrassment, silently praying for the expurgated version, rather than having to suffer the fully-detailed, blow-by-blow ringside coverage, with inter-round commentaries by W. Barrington Dalby, like the boxing matches Da used to listen to on the radio.

Certain less-than-generous companions over the years have suggested that I stopped growing UP very shortly afterwards, but this I can deny with absolute certainty, as it took twenty-ish years of copious spud consumption to get me to the towering (not quite) five-foot-one I have so far attained.

The year was 1947, which is still talked about in the welly-and-dung-graip community as the worst winter since Methuselah's goat was a kid, with the country 'oxter deep' in snow for months, and brass monkeys queuing up outside the blacksmiths every morning, with the family jewels in a shopping bag. However, I was blissfully unaware of all this, as I was born in mid-January, one week before the 'big snow' really came on, in Tower Hill Hospital, on the outskirts of Armagh City.

I was christened immediately, in the hospital, as I was a sickly six-pounder, and due to my condition, and Ma's advanced age, I was not expected to 'do'. So far I managed to defy medical opinion, although after watching the fate of Bobby Ewing in 'Dallas', I cannot rule out the possibility that all this is really a dream, and that I only exist as a figment of my own imagination.

My father used to tell the story of the wake where the corpse sat up in the bed, looked around at the assembled company, and said, "What the blazes is going on here? Sure I'm not dead!" He was immediately told, rather forcefully, (no doubt by men drunk enough to be certain of their facts!) "Lie down there, man! Sure the doctor knows more than you do!"

Hopefully mine did not.

The Mammy.

The Mammy in question was Annie Rooney, from near Clea, 'out beyont' Keady, and she only managed a height of about four foot ten herself, so it is hardly surprising that none of her family made the grade as professional basketball players. She was a small, round, dark-haired woman, well used to hard work, and a lifetime of 'stretching a pound till it squealed'. She was brought up on a small, rocky farm at the upper end of Clea Lake, (they seem to spell it 'Clay' nowadays) or the 'Head o' the Lough', as she used to call it, with one younger sister Bridget, and two older brothers, Mick and Charlie.

She used to walk up the Mountainy Road and across the fields to Clea School, a tiny two-room building, (one room for the girls, one for the boys) where every pupil had to bring a lump of coal for the fire each day in the winter. She took us to see it a few times, and told us tales of walking barefoot to school in the summer, with a gang of kids, all singing -

> 'Clea scholars behind the wall,
> A pint of pish would drown them all,
> A penny candle would show them light,
> From early morning till late at night'

They don't write songs like that any more, do they? And if they did, they would probably get an ASBO for it, or a grant from the Arts Council.

Her father died in the great flu epidemic of 1919, which killed more people in one year than the Great War had killed in four. I can almost hear God singing 'Anything you can do, I can do better'! I think Granda Rooney had three small farms in the Clea and Derrynoose area at the time of his death, but these were gradually sold off over the years to support the family, as the sons' aptitude for farming was poor, and only scaled the dizzy heights of mediocrity on rare occasions. Times were hard, so Annie and Bridget were dispatched to the 'Big City' of Armagh around 1929, to find work, and (more importantly) send money home, to help keep the two brothers in the state that most Irish mothers of the period thought their sons were entitled to. Her mother survived until the 1950s, but the two brothers never married, and both are now dead, so the Rooney branch of the family has died out completely.

Ma worked in Miss Bleakley's Hotel, in Scotch St, for the next ten years or so, a place she really liked, but Bridget moved around more, in domestic service, and seldom got a place where the conditions, or the food, were as good.

Ma's oft repeated claim to fame from this period was the fact that she used to carry dinners to Harold Courtney, who was hanged for murder in the 1930s. He was held on the equivalent of 'Death Row' in Armagh jail while awaiting execution, and was therefore entitled to better food than the rest of the inmates, so his dinner was sent from the hotel each day, wrapped up in a basket, and delivered to the warder at the prison door. I suppose she was Armagh's first low-tech delivery service – the 'Pizza-Certainly-Not-Express' of the pre-war era! Murder was such a rare event in those days that a song was written about it, detailing the awful deed, and the consequences that inevitably followed -

> "My name is Harold Courtney,
> in Armagh Jail I lie,
> For the murder of poor Minnie Reid,
> a crime I can't deny"

Ma knew it off by heart, of course, and would break into it at the least provocation, in spite of the fact that she could not carry a tune in a bucket, and had a voice like a corncrake with tonsillitis - a trait, incidentally, that appears to have formed a major part of my own inheritance. My efforts at singing were often described by Da, (who was a noted singer in his youth) as slightly less melodic than a 'goat pilling on a can lid'. My own children, who in later years had to suffer my efforts to 'cheer up' numerous car journeys, will testify to this at the drop of a hat! After a verse or two of 'Me and Bobby McGee', they might not know where Baton Rouge was, but they reckoned the sooner I was 'busted flat' in it, the better!

The two Miss Bleakleys retired to Bangor around the end of the thirties, so the hotel was closed, and Ma moved on to work in Dougans, on the Moy Rd. She worked there right through the war years, and she was again lucky in finding a place where the food and the treatment were excellent. She always talked about running into the fields in her nightclothes when the air-raid sirens went off, and seeing the refugees getting off the trains in Armagh, after the bombing in Belfast. At this stage of the war, everyone expected the entire German Parachute Corps to land in the back garden at any time, (all dressed as nuns, of course!) and Hitler to come goose-stepping down English Street in person, to get his funny moustache trimmed at the barbers. The way Ma described it, twenty years later; she still seemed vaguely surprised that he hadn't!

Her sister Bridget used to come over to see her in Dougans, to 'get a dacent bite to ate' at times, for her own place of work, like many others at the time, was not noted for fattening up the domestic staff. Sadly, it was not enough to improve her failing health, and Bridget died in 1944.

Tom Dougan owned a small farm at Drummondmore, about a mile outside the town, occupied by Willie McFadden and his wife, an elderly couple from Co. Antrim. She was a tiny, stoutish woman, with a head of pure white hair, tied in a bun, and always dressed in black, with a black shawl around her shoulders. Her husband was just the opposite - a long, thin, gangly old man, slightly bent by that age, who would have been tall enough to 'ate hay off a half-loft' when he was 'at himself'. Willie used to keep an eye on the farm, but was really retired, and would often disappear to town to 'get a few messages' for the wife, in his best pinstriped suit and soft hat. He might appear back with only half the list of goods, saying "it wisnae forrad, Hen" ('Ballymena spake' for "Sadly, they did not have it in stock, Dearest") so that he might be able to escape the eagle eye of the missus for a while tomorrow as well, and maybe sample a 'wee drop of the craythur' before coming home.

Ma was dispatched to Drummondmore each day in the haymaking or harvest time, a walk of about a mile along the old railway line, to assist Mrs McFadden making food for the gang of men who descended on the place at such times. It was here that she met my father, in the summer of 1945.

M'Da

Da was John Rafferty, the youngest of five surviving children, (I think there had been eight in total) born on a much smaller farm at the Flush, about a mile on the Armagh side of Loughgall. He was known as 'Red Jack', on account of his ginger hair, and to distinguish him from 'Black Jack', another John Rafferty (a cousin) from the same area. He was only about five and a half feet tall, but broad shouldered, and very strong, and could use a scythe, spade, pitchfork, or bow saw with equal skill all day without any difficulty, usually whistling or singing at the same time, with the 'sweat flying aff him' in all directions.

His mother died when he was very young, and the 'Oul Boy' married again, so the first wife's family were turfed out, as often happened, to ensure that the second wife's family 'got the place'. The 'place' in question was no Texas Cattle Ranch, and had barely enough land to make a decent football field, but evidently this was not a consideration! Da had to go into hospital for a few days at the age of about twelve, to get some warts removed from the back of his neck, and was walking home - as he thought – when he met his father in the horse and cart. Far from the lift home he was expecting, he was told that his bed had been dumped out, and he was no longer considered to be 'on the ration strength'!

He was 'took in' by his oldest sister, Caroline Fox, who lived a mile or so up the road towards Armagh, in a cottage at Annacramp. Her husband, John, worked on the railway, and Da lived with them for some years, working for Willie Armstrong, at his farm in Drummondmore, a couple of miles away. John Fox was transferred to Newry in the late 1920s, and the family moved to a railwayman's cottage out the Warrenpoint road, so Da went to live in Armstrong's full time. As an unmarried 'sarvint boy', he had a bed in the hayloft, a far more comfortable arrangement than it might sound, as it was warm, dry, and well insulated from the winter winds. It must have been a 'good billet', as he stayed for twenty years, and he often talked about the great times he had in Armstrong's, for the craic was ninety, the grub was good, and the boss was 'a dacent man', features that were often more noticeable for their absence in the hungry thirties.

He used get the half day off on a Saturday, wash and shave in the wee stream that ran past the farmyard, and head into Armagh for the afternoon. He often sat on the Mall wall and watched the cricket, and then went to the pictures in the Cosy Corner in Russell St, or the 'flea pit' as it was usually known. He sometimes rode his bike to Warrenpoint, to visit the Fox family for the weekend, which was a day's work in itself. The roads were a lot worse than they are now, and the bog standard black boneshaker of those days was a far cry from the ultra-light streamlined techno-bikes of today. The 'good suit and flat cap' would hardly be as aerodynamic as the multi-coloured florescent outfits (with padded 'seating area'!) you see the cyclists in these days either!

Da was known as 'a great man for the reading', another feature that I have inherited, and was especially fond of cowboy books, and 'good juicy murders'. Armstrong's was just across the fields from the railway crossing at

Reilly's Rocks, where Gerald Rafferty, the journalist and author, was brought up. They were not related, but Da used to be great friends with Gerry, and his brothers, Barney and Paddy, and often featured in Gerry's weekly column in the Ireland's Saturday Night in later years. Gerry told the story of 'Red Jack' coming to get him to play the fiddle at a wedding near Loughgall, where the cow calved in the middle of the proceedings, and the entire wedding party, fiddler and all, moved to the byre and continued the festivities - a story I often heard re-told when I was young. We used to get the Ireland's Saturday Night newspaper every week without fail, and Ma turned to Gerry's column straight away, to check if Da was mentioned, or any of the neighbours we knew. Gerry later produced a book of stories of country life, called 'The Band Played On', and the tale of the 'dance in the byre' was in that as well.

There was a large hay meadow near Dougan's farm, and several farmers had strips of land in it, marked out with holes dug at the corners. (And woe betide anyone who cut an extra swathe over and above his allotted area!) Sometimes several people cut hay at the same time, and all piled in together to help build it into stacks, etc, and it was at one of these communal gatherings my Ma and Da first met, in 1945. He was just over forty, and she was thirty-seven, so they wasted no time, and they were married in January 1946. The honeymoon was a day trip to Dublin, the farthest either of them had ever been, as far as I know, and the farthest either of them had ever went, until Ma came to visit me in Scotland, thirty years later. I don't think a fortnight in Florida or the Seychelles was mentioned, even at the planning stage, and there was no stag night in Prague or Bangkok either. Armstrong's hayloft was no place for a bride, so they moved in to one room of the farm at Drummondmore with the McFaddens. Da got a new job, in Henry Bleakley's nursery at Killuney corner, about a mile outside Armagh, on the Portadown Road, where he stayed another twenty years. A grand worker, but not what you would call footloose!

2 THE PLACE

In 'The Green Fool', Patrick Kavanagh talks of being born into a leaky thatched cottage in the stony hills of Monaghan, with a converted onion box for a cradle. Being born into North Armagh, of course, my cradle was a converted apple box, but the rest rings a bell. A younger sister, called Bridget, was born just over a year later.

Willie McFadden died sometime around this period, so Mrs McFadden moved into one room of the wee house, and we took over the rest, as the old lady's health began to deteriorate. I can vaguely remember her, with snow-white hair tied up in a bun, a long black dress and black shawl, hobbling about on a stick. She taught me my first poem -

> Maggie Pickens had a coo,
> Black an' white abeen the broo,
> Open the gate an' let her through,
> Maggie Pickens ain coo!

It would probably be lauded as an Ulster Scots Cultural Treasure nowadays, but back then it was just the way she talked. For the benefit of those who do not 'spake Ulstir', a 'coo' is Ballymena talk for a cow, evidently a Friesian, as it was 'black and white' above the brow! She moved to London shortly afterwards, to live with her daughter, leaving us in sole charge of the house and farm. Her daughter had been a 'clippie' on the London buses during the war, and had married a soldier from Poland, one of the refugees who escaped from Hitler, to continue the fight from Britain. Mrs McFadden did not get along with him, and always referred to him as the 'Oul Buck'. They had a son a few years older than me, who was a great Tottenham Hotspur fan, and sent me Spurs photos and stuff. I am still a mild Spurs supporter to this day - 'fan' (i.e. fanatic) sounds a bit too enthusiastic for me. Such are the accidental connections that so often influence our lives!

The farm was about fourteen acres, with about four acres under the plough at that time, and the rest in grazing, or hay. It was the last house at the end of a tiny, winding, half-mile long lane, with hedges high enough to meet above your head, and was hidden behind an embankment of the old Armagh-Newry railway line, close to where the great railway disaster of 1889 occurred. The nearest other dwellings were at least a quarter-mile away, and out of sight behind the hill, or the railway bank, so it felt like being completely isolated from the rest of civilization - in time as well as space, for we were like a tiny enclave of the 19th century, (or maybe even the 18th century!) surrounded by a world that was painfully struggling into the second half of the 20th. Da often described it as living in the 'the arsehole of nowhere', and it certainly felt like that at times, but to me, it was the most wonderful place it was possible to grow up in.

The house had a wee porch, and a half-door, opening into a hall with a jamb wall. There were two small rooms to the left, (the gable end of the house), and a big kitchen with a stone flagged floor to the right, with one larger bedroom off it. The kitchen had a huge open hearth, with a 'crook' and two hobs at the side, all of it spectacularly soot-blackened, and wonderful for making soda bread and pancakes on the griddle. Wonderful, that is, if you were on the eating end of the operation, but probably less so for the one doing the baking. It had an old-fashioned dresser, against the wall opposite the fireplace, with willow pattern plates standing up on the shelves, and two tables opposite one another - a small square one, holding crocks of milk, buckets of spring water, bread bins, and similar assorted necessities, against the front wall, and a much bigger, 'scrubbed to operating-theatre standard' pine table, for eating, making butter, rolling out dough for soda farls, playing cards, and anything else that needed doing. There was a big barrel churn on four legs that sat in the corner when not in use, and a long horsehair sofa against the jamb wall, which everyone sat on most of the time, as there was a 'draught that would clean corn' round the back of the ankles if you sat between the fire and the door. There were two hobs on either side of the fireplace, where boots (or anything else) could be left to dry, and various cooking utensils, such as a griddle, three-legged pot, frying pan, etc, were hung on the side, or hidden in the cupboard to the right of the chimney brace. The smoothing iron was a hollow metal triangle, with a removable inside part of solid iron, which was put in the fire until it was red-hot. It was then lifted out with tongs, and put into the main part, which, being metal also, became quite hot very quickly, and had a wooden handle to protect the user from the heat when ironing.

The house and out-buildings were all in one long line, on a slight hillside, with a cobbled area we called 'the front street' along the front, and a steeper fall towards a small stream at the bottom of the hill. It was all mud-wall, and the thatch was a yard thick, so it was warm and comfortable when the fire was blazing up the chimney, but was inclined to leak copiously in heavy rain. The 'low room' had a slight slope, and a small lake used to accumulate in the lowest corner after a really wet night. I used to take my children, and later my grandchildren, to the Ulster Folk Museum at Cultra, and see houses just like the one I was brought up in, except they were in far better condition!

The barn, stable and byre, on the other hand, had a corrugated tin roof, which did not leak at all - a reminder of the relative importance of us and the animals in the Great Cosmic Plan, perhaps? The barn had a selection of ancient agricultural implements that you only see in museums these days - a scythe (that I was forbidden to touch), a thistle puller (that I had to use all-too-often), a turnip pulper (to cut up feed for the horse), and a two-man cross-cut saw, (that I helped Da with on several occasions) amongst others. It had a set of scales for hundredweight bags of spuds, and special 'spud shovel' for lifting them, like a curved graip with a rim around the outside. A huge open hayshed stood behind the house, in an enclosed 'haggard' - it seemed to hold about three million bales of hay, and I have seen it full, (and helped to fill it, in fact!) many times. There was a tarred lean-to wooden henhouse 'tacked on' to one gable, to keep Brer Fox away from the chooks. It had a 'clap till' tarred wooden door – ie. it was loosely attached at one side, and was closed by lifting it across the entrance, (ie 'clapped' against the frame) where it was held in place by the only totally dependable elements in the agricultural universe – gravity and baler twine.

The 'facilities' consisted of a much smaller tin shack, also located in the yard, with slightly less secure 'clap till' sheet of tin for a door, and a supply of torn up pages from the Irish News for the use of its patrons. Not exactly Kittensoft, I can assure you - thon Labrador pup on TV would have wound up toothless if he tried taking any liberties with our toilet paper! It was not designed to encourage 'all night sittings' either, as the wind coming under the door would 'freeze your assets' quicker than the PSNI Fraud Squad.

The water supply was a spring well, with beautiful cool, clear water, and amply supplied with frogs - the only drawback was that it was about two or three hundred yards from the house! Two big white enamel buckets of water had to be carried home every day, a chore that was passed on to me when I was old enough to lift them. The route ran down to the stream, over the 'kesh', (a wee bridge made of railway-sleepers) and across the field to the well, at the foot of the hill opposite the house. I had to stop and put the buckets down to rest every fifty yards or so, and the field often contained a number of large bullocks, so I usually had a close escort of very nosey beef snorting behind me, and sniffing the water buckets, before I got very far.

We had no electricity anywhere near the place, as it was a half mile from the main road, so our only light was a tiny oil lamp, or a hurricane lamp for going outside. There were far fewer street lights in those days, so 'dark' in the country really was dark, compared to what it is now, and it did mean you could see the moon and the stars really well. The Milky Way was amazingly clear, and I seem to remember the Aurora Borealis, or Northern Lights, being very bright in the 1950s, and very common, (Da used to call them the 'Rory Bory Ellis'!) but I did not really see them as clearly again until quite recently. We got a Tilley lamp when I was six or eight, which had a gauze mantle, and was pumped up, so that the paraffin was delivered to it under pressure. The light was much greater, and did not flicker like the oil lamp, so we were all hugely impressed with the marvels of modern technology!

The recent 'Victorian Farm' programme on the TV brought back a lot of memories – a lot of what they did, and how they did it, was all too familiar, even though we were supposed to be sixty or seventy years on from when they were meant to be living. Most of our clothes were 'store bought', but Ma did knit a lot of socks, and darned them with wool and a big needle, when they got holes in the heels. There seemed to be an endless supply of thick woollen jumpers, which were also mended and re-mended until the patched bits were twice as thick as the original. Much of the housework, such as cooking, butter making, washing, etc, was exactly as done in the TV series, and much of the farm work was very similar

The 'Bastes'

The four-legged occupants consisted of one small red cow, a few calves and bullocks, a cat or two to harass the rodent population, and a big brown carthorse called Charlie, with huge hairy feet, and a backbone like a ridge of the Matterhorn. He was a very friendly giant, however, with big lips that could have lifted sugar lumps from the smallest of hands without so much as the tiniest nip. I was placed on his back on many occasions, coming back from the fields, hanging on to his mane while Da led him by the halter, and still remember the elevated view of the world to this day. Not to mention the stabbing pains in the rear end, from his backbone!

We had a couple of dozen hens, and a rooster who would have 'lit on ye', if you were not careful. He regarded the back yard as his personal property, and would attack anything or anyone he saw as a threat to his domain. He even flew up unto Ma's back and dug his claws into her shoulders on one occasion, and learned a harsh lesson in the process - Ma was not exactly built like a sprinter, but could exhibit an amazing turn of speed with an 'ash plant' in her hand, and murder in her heart, as we kids also found out to our cost, on more than one occasion! He and I had a sort of 'armed neutrality' pact, as I never ventured near him without a stick for self defence, and we would circle round each other, eyes locked, like two 'hard' blokes in a pub trying to impress their girlfriends without actually getting hit.

We also reared pheasants for a few years, by setting a clutch of eggs under a 'clocking' hen, to get them hatched out. We had to keep them in a netting wire cage, as they were better flyers than the chickens, and would have been impossible to keep track of had they been on the loose. I remember a fox getting in on one occasion, and committing considerable mayhem before making his escape. I have no idea where the pheasants went to after they grew up, but they were only reared for the shooting season, presumably it was 'a short life and a merry one' for most of them.

We always had a few dogs as well, as Da was in the Beagle club, and kept a couple of 'good hunters', and sometimes looked after dogs for other members who were less rurally situated. I remember we looked after a big Kerry Blue terrier for an Armagh man for a while, which had to be kept securely tied up, as it 'wud've ate ye' had it been let loose. I think it had taken a mouthful of somebody when it lived in town, and got a suspended sentence – it was scheduled for an appointment with a bag, a block, and a quarry hole if it tried to sample anyone else!

Da used to milk the cow and feed the calves before cycling the half mile to work for 8am every morning, and do the same again after he came home at 6pm in the evenings. He did any ploughing, harvesting, and haymaking as well, after his normal job, and seemed to spend huge amounts of time sawing up logs for firewood in his 'spare time'!

Tom Dougan, the farm owner, was retired, but used to dander out the disused railway line from town most days, to do any other jobs, and keep an eye on the livestock. He would put Charlie the horse in the cart about once a week or so, and drive into Armagh to get any messages needed. On more than one occasion, he fell asleep on the way home, and the horse delivered him safely into the yard, stuck his huge head in over the half door, and neighed at Ma to come out and waken the driver. Progress be damned - show me the GPS that will do that for you! No doubt Charlie had kept to his own side of the road the whole way home, and probably stuck his hoof out to 'indicate' before turning into our lane.

When I got to 4 or 5 years old, I used to accompany Tom on some of these expeditions, sitting on the front seat like 'Lord Muck from Clabber Hill', and picturing myself as 'riding shotgun' on the Deadwood Stage, with hostile Injuns and 'hold-up merchants' concealed behind every tree on the road. Da was a great Western reader, so I was familiar with expressions such as 'go fer yer hardware, ya son-of-a-gun', 'hit the trail, Pardner' and 'Adios, Amigo' from a very early age. 'Adios' was pronounced 'addy-oats', of course, by all the kids around Armagh, whose knowledge of colloquial Mexican in the 1950s (gained in the stalls of the local cinemas), left a lot to be desired! We once went to Willie John Ross's forge, on the Loughgall Road, to get the horse shod, and I can still remember the blacksmith with his apron, and asking him if 'Poor Charlie' was getting hurt by the nails going into his hoof. Charlie himself, of course, just stood there patiently, lifting each massive hoof as instructed, with a lot more forbearance than I would have showed when forced by Ma into a shoe shop

3 BEING A WE'AN

Mrs McFadden used to call us all 'weans', being from Ballymena direction, and therefore a speaker of what they now call 'Ulster-Scots'. I think it is just a contraction of 'wee ones'. Separate language? My arse, as the great English philosopher Jim Royle used to say!

'Near Kilt'

When Da was due home, I used to walk halfway out the lane to meet him, and get a ride home on the bar of his bike. I used to wait under the old railway bridge, about a quarter of a mile from the house, totally alone, something that it would be hard to imagine a 4-year old being allowed to do these days. One evening, he had just put me on the bar, and was in the act of throwing his leg over the bike, when the front forks broke, and the whole front wheel assembly just collapsed under us. I got a busted lip, and Da a few bruises, but very little else. We were just starting off down a bit of a hill, so if it had broken thirty seconds later, we would have been near the bottom, going fast, with high hedges on both sides, and a very loose, stony surface underneath - a much nastier fall. Ma did her usual Oscar-winning-disaster-movie 'yis all cudda bin kilt' routine, and that put a stop to my bike riding for a while.

This was the scariest part of the lane, with thick hawthorn hedges so tall that they almost met overhead, and really dark in the winter nights. Ma often told us about her and Da coming home late one winter's night, before I was born, and heard a strange clanking noise, like dragging chains, as they came through the old bridge. As they walked on, the chains seemed to be dragging towards them up the darkest part of the lane, and then a white 'something' appeared, bobbing about in mid-air, three or four feet above the ground! They froze in mid step, as the apparition approached, the clanking getting ever louder as it got nearer! Ma later swore that if she had been alone, she would have beaten Roger Bannister to the 4-minute mile record, utterly convinced it was a ghost. Da, however, was less excitable, and walked on towards it, albeit more slowly.

It turned out to be the horse, which had not been unhitched properly earlier in the day, and still had a chain attached to his collar. The 'ghost' was the white blaze on his face, bobbing about as he walked. I've often wondered how many of those authentic, guaranteed, 'no doubt whatsoever it was a ghost' stories you used to hear got started in the same way.

DIY Carpentry

Ma had to go to town once a week to do the shopping, and sometimes Tom Dougan used to mind us, as he would be out and about the farm in the afternoon. This was not always a total success, as he was in his 70s by then, and if he sat down by the kitchen fire, he would often fall asleep, leaving us free to do absolutely anything that two adventurous three and four year-olds could think of to pass the time. On one occasion, Ma came home to find us dressed in a very odd assortment of clothes, and - after some persuasion - managed to get him to admit that we had been 'paddling' in the horse's drinking water, and he had to change us from the skin out. This might seem like a fairly trivial task to a 'Nineties Man', reared on pram pushing, nappy changing, and 'getting in touch with his feminine side', but to the male of the species in the early 1950s (especially one born in the 1880s) children in general, and children's clothes in particular, would have been a complete mystery.

On another famous occasion, we escaped again, and decided to experiment with a little carpentry, using Da's trusty bow saw. Now, as anyone who has tried it will tell you, the one-manpower bow saw is not an easy implement to master, as you really need to work it one handed, and hold the log steady with the other hand, something far beyond our limited strength. I have seen my own children, and now grandchildren, trying to use one, and suffering exactly the same difficulties - pushing the saw and holding it upright is hard enough, but it is even harder to get something to co-operate by staying still long enough to be sawed. However, we had a big advantage they did not - we had seen a crosscut in action. All we needed was a steady log, and Bob's Your Uncle. And we found one, almost at once - the shaft of the cart! Bridget got one side, I got the other, and we were over half way through the shaft before Tom woke up, and prevented a total disaster.

He took full responsibility, saying it was entirely his fault, and after all, it was his cart, and pleaded for leniency from the court - mostly in vain, for Ma hit the roof, and us, in about equal measure. I doubt if Perry Mason himself could have got us off, not even if Paul Drake turned up with six new witnesses, and a guilty-looking bloke with sawdust in the turn-ups of his trousers on the last day of the trial. There was no 'Let the Little Darlings Express Themselves' nonsense in those days, I can tell you!

Tom got a man to glue some wood into the cut, and bolt on two railway fishplates either side, the same way as they are used to join the rails together, and made a sound job of it, but we were never allowed to forget our foray into the carpentry trade, and spent more time in the doghouse than the beagles did over the next few weeks

'Drappin' Spuds.

One of my earliest memories is of planting spuds in the three-acre field beside the house, when I could not have been much more than four years old. Da had prepared the drills, using the horse and a single drill plough, and then we spread dung in them from the back of the horse's cart. This was a backbreaking job, as the manure had to be lifted from the 'duncle', (strategically placed - a dung-graip's throw from the byre door) and loaded into the cart, which would have been two or three feet off the ground. Thousand-horsepower tractors with a front-end loader were not even a gleam in some futuristic designer's eye at the time, so the only answer was the traditional one-manpower dung-graip, and a good pair of wellies. Preferably hole-less wellies –

any tiny opening could result in a sock-full of highly aromatic duncle seepage, and even the most unflappable of farmer's wives would draw the line at letting socks like that across the threshold. At least you were guaranteed to be warm – if the work was not hard enough, the steam rising from the freshly opened dung-heap could persuade even the most traditional countryman to take off his jacket, but NEVER, of course, his cap!

The horse then walked up the drills, stopping every few paces, to allow the dung to be lifted, one graip at a time, from the back of the cart, and dropped into the drills at suitable intervals. Five or six drills could be done at a time - within easy graip-throwing range from a central position – and the horse yelled at to 'walk on' or 'whoa' when required. When the back of the cart was cleared, the man might have to climb in, and throw the stuff out from within the cart.

Woe betide the man who had an impatient horse – if it moved, and jerked the cart in mid-throw, the thrower might be hurled 'on his mouth and nose' into the pile of dung left in the cart, or (even worse) thrown arse-over-tip out over the back unto the ground. This could be a painful and very dangerous experience, especially as he would be holding a graip in his hand at the time! Being too small to shovel the stuff, I used to sit on the seat of the cart, holding the reins, with instructions NOT to even twitch them, on pain of death, in case the horse took this as an instruction to 'walk on', and deposited Da in a heap along with the manure.

The best bit was driving from the duncle to the field and back, for the shoveller got a few minutes rest, and no actual driving was involved, as the horse knew the routine better than us after two or three runs. The main thing was, I got to do the 'driving' - well, to hold the reins, at least, to foster the delusion that I was actually having some influence on the direction we were taking!

The clumps of dung then had to be spread, using the graip, more or less evenly along the drills, ready for the actual planting. Seed spuds came in hessian bags, and were 'dropped' by hand, a foot to eighteen inches apart, in the bottom of the drills. Some people used buckets, bags, or similar items to carry a load of spuds along with them, but the most common way was the 'bag apron'. A hessian bag was cut open, and one end tied around the waist, using the obligatory baler twine, without which the entire agricultural industry would (quite literally!) fall apart. The other end of the bag hung loose, and the user held this in one hand, and filled the resulting three-cornered 'bag' with seed spuds. Thus the dropper's waist took most of the weight, and the other hand was free to lift a fistful of spuds from the bag, and place them in the bottom of the drill, at the required spacing. A good dropper could almost manage walking pace, while bent 'two-double'. It was called 'dropping', but actually dropping them was not approved of - some degree of precision was required, it seemed, and anyone not bent 'two double' was soon given a sharp 'flea in the ear'. I don't think it mattered that much to the spuds, but if anyone saw a spud crop coming up unevenly, it was something of an embarrassment to the farmer, and the subsequent work of grubbing, 'running up', etc, to keep the weeds down, became much more difficult.

Even at the age of four or five my sister and I were roped in to help, as Ma would have been doing a lot of the dropping, and we were easier to mind when we were in the same place. It was a lot cheaper than a day nursery and a lot more exciting for us as well, and we did get a surprising amount of spuds plonked in more or less the right place. Da would have started off the first few drills with us, but when we got a bit of a head start, he would go and hitch up the horse to the drill plough, to 'cover' them. This was another physically tiring, and skilful job, as the ploughman had to exert a fair amount of pressure on the plough handles to keep it splitting the furrow exactly down the middle, while holding the horse's reins loosely as it walked down the drill. Even turning round on the 'head-rig' required a lot of pulling and hauling at the plough, and backing and forwarding with the horse. A horse who 'knew the ropes' was essential, as he had to walk the furrows straight, or they would make a total mess of all the hard work done to get to that stage. I can remember standing in a furrow watching as they passed by within a couple of feet, the horse a huge animal whose belly I could have comfortably walked under, and Da with the sweat flying off him, in his usual well-faded blue dungarees, and 'duncher' cap, which never left his head, except at bedtime. Although I can't actually confirm that - he may well have slept in it too!

Faded denim with patches and rips is considered a 'fashion statement' these days, but back then it was a sign of too little spare cash. In fact, it was more of a lifestyle statement - a farmer going out to a hiring fair always looked for a man with patches on the knees of his overalls. If the patches were on the arse instead, it showed he spent too much time sitting down, and was not worth hiring. A pair of dungarees with all the pockets in place, and no patches or rips, was a rare sight, even amongst the more affluent farmers. Appearance was not something a man wasted his money on, and the thought of buying new clothes just because the old ones had gone out of fashion (even by 10 years!) would have given any farmer palpitations, if not a full heart attack.

Your true 1950s Culshie, or 'Munchie' as they are often called round Armagh, would never remove any clothing, no matter how hot. 'If it keeps out the cold, it will keep out the heat', I was often told, by men wearing huge hob-nailed boots, corduroy breeches, tied at the knees with baler twine, thick vest, heavy long-sleeved collarless shirt, thick waistcoat, and heavy jacket, making hay on a July day that would scorch the paint off the hinges of the gates of Hell. They might remove the jacket, if actually experiencing breathing difficulties, but never the 'weskit', or the hat. These young farmers nowadays, driving about in shorts and sun-glasses, bronzed like California Beach-Bums, in their huge tractors, with music blaring from the stereo, must have a lot of their forefathers turning in their graves!

Even a place as backward as ours was not totally immune from the 20th century, as a few years later we got a neighbouring farmer in with a 'Wee Grey Fergie' tractor, and a spud dropper on the back. This was an amazing piece of modern technology (to us, anyway), as you sat on the back, with a big tray of spuds in front of you, and dropped one down the chute every time the bell went 'ding'. You could even adjust the 'ding' for how far apart you wanted them, for 'earlies' or 'main crop' planting. The machine did the covering as well, so the reduction in work was amazing, and the feeling of riding on the back of the tractor, and being lifted out on the hydraulics at the end of every drill was a great thrill to a kid from the stone-age like me.

The other part of the job was digging the spuds out again, in the autumn, which was an even bigger operation, involving a squad of people arranged in twos or threes up the drill. The inevitable 'Wee Grey Fergie' tractor with a potato digger ran up the drill, so that the plough part got under the spuds, and the spinner at the back would scatter the soil and spuds across a yard or two of the ground already dug. As this machine passed each pair of gatherers, they dropped in behind it, and 'scrabbed' the spuds from the soil, into a metal mesh 'pirta basket', which were then emptied into the usual hessian bags when full. If you had enough gatherers, the tractor man could be kept moving all day, as the start of the drill would be cleared, ready for him, by the time he got the top done, and come back round again. This resulted in a lot of people with their bums in the air, and presented an irresistible target for the younger gatherers, and often some of the sneakier older ones as well. A skelp on the arse with a big spud was not that funny to the receiver, especially when they jumped up and looked around, to see only an entire field full of totally innocent and very industrious workers, with no indication whatsoever as to who might be the guilty party. All they could do was bend down once more, and wait for the inevitable follow-up, in the hope that they might spot the culprit on his repeat performance. A balance had to be struck between letting the lads have a little fun, and letting it degenerate into a full scale 'cloddin' session, before total chaos ensued.

The Slipe

One implement that was definitely not 20th century was the slipe, the only other example of which I have seen is in the Transport Museum at Cultra. The museum begins with the 'most primitive form of transport', just inside the door - the 'Y-shaped branch hauled behind a horse, with a few animal skins tied across it', and I think the slipe is in there as second most primitive, right next to it! It was a kind of six-foot-ish-long sled, about three feet wide, and two feet deep, with iron runners, and was made of substantial planks, built to stand up to a lot of heavy work hauling stones, etc. We got permission to use some stones from the disused railway line nearby to repair the lane, and our next-door neighbour, Tam McKernan, used our horse and slipe to haul them. I was about five at the time, and was widely considered (by me at least) to be chief engineer on the project. It took ages, as each load only did about two or three yards of lane, the lane was a full half-mile long from the road to our house, and none of us (certainly not Tam, or the horse) were in any great hurry. We would go up on the railway embankment, find an area where the stones were loose, and shovel in a slipe-full, Tam with a long-tailed shovel, and me with an old cut-down spade. I would sit on the front of the slipe, (as befitted the chief engineer) and he would walk alongside, driving the horse, and haul them to the lane, where they had to be shovelled out, and spread evenly across the pathway.

Tam was known as a 'rough man on tools' - if he got his hands on a spade or shovel in the morning, it seldom survived beyond dinnertime. If he didn't break the handle out of it, he would probably break the head off it. He was a tall, thin bachelor of middle age, with the obligatory dungarees and cap, but always wore a proper shirt and a tie, (and sometimes he even had shiny shoes!), and lived with his mother in a small farm halfway down the lane. His mother was a tiny woman, who had been about four years old at the time of the Armagh railway disaster in 1889. She had been due to go on the train, which was taking a load of kids on a Sunday school trip to Warrenpoint. There was too big a load to pull up the hill from Armagh towards Markethill, so they left half the carriages on the hill, and pulled the rest to the top. However, the brakes did not hold, and the carriages began to run back down the hill, gathering speed all the time. Another train coming up from Armagh crashed into the runaway carriages, smashing them to matchwood, and killing many of the children inside. Mrs McKernan had taken sick some days before, and was kept at home, with much wailing, and complaining, but several of her companions were amongst the dead. Strange that she ended up living to a ripe old age, less than half a mile from where she might well have been killed, had she not been sick as a child!

Tam considered himself a great pipe smoker, but the rest of the country considered him a great match burner, and an even greater talker. He would start a conversation, drag out the pipe, clean it out with a spike on the end of his penknife, cut up the tobacco, pack it in, and expend about ten matches getting it going, talking all the time. He would then use the pipe as a pointer to emphasize his opinion, waving it around for several minutes at a time, as he got carried away. When he paused for breath long enough to try another puff, he often found the pipe was out, and he had to get the matches out again. He did not spend much on tobacco, but matches cost him a fortune! His whole life was devoted to the rituals of the pipe smoker - cleaning it out, filling it, lighting it, emptying it, digging things out of it with a sharp instrument, putting it in his top pocket, getting it out again, etc, etc, all for a few mouthfuls of nicotine. Da used to say he would need a bread poultice on the back of his neck, to help him draw the pipe, the amount of effort that went into getting it started, and it was widely believed that he had shares in Swan Vesta.

This was a major impediment on the stone hauling job, of course, as people from Armagh used to take their walks along the old railway lines, to exercise themselves, or their dogs. Any passer-by was an excuse for Tam to get the pipe lit up, and sit on the corner of the slipe for a half hour, giving the person the benefit of his experience, on any subject the unfortunate punter had happened to mention. Local or national, international diplomacy or scientific research, horse racing or football – no subject was off limits, and Tam had the inside line on all of them, and was more than willing to share his expertise, whether the recipient wanted it or not.

Green ear prevention.

We kids had no fear of the horse, or any of the animals whatsoever, regardless of their size. We just assumed that the people were in charge, and the animals did what they were told, and as long as you were sufficiently confident about that, they usually did! Even at four or five I would have had no qualms about setting off alone to bring in the cow, and 'tie her up' in the byre ready for milking, even though I might have to climb on an upturned bucket to reach the chain over her neck, and lean right under her to secure it. The wee cow had fantastically curved horns, (Da actually had to saw the end of one of them off with a hacksaw, to prevent it growing into her eye!) and I sometimes used to grab on to one of them to climb up to reach the chain for her neck. Da milked her by hand, into a big galvanised bucket, and I was called upon to assist at times, in the prevention of 'green ear'. This was caused by the cow flicking her tail around to brush off the flies, and if she had been careless about what she lay in, or was suffering from 'thin and greenish motions' the end of it could be rather messy. On these occasions, I might be detailed to stand behind the cow, holding the end of the tail, to prevent her slapping Da up the ear with it as he leaned against her while milking. It seemed that 'green hand' on my part was less important than 'green ear' on his! Some cows might have kicked at this kind of indignity, but our wee red Dexter was so quiet, she never said a word.

The Cookstown man

As a 'one cow' ranch, we did not keep a bull, so the Artificial Insemination man, from the Ministry of Agriculture Office in Cookstown, was called in whenever the cow was 'on the notion'. He was referred to as 'The Cookstown Man', or the 'Bull in the Bowler Hat', but as a child, I knew nothing of the reason for these visits, so he was regarded as a sort of Santa Claus for adults. No doubt many modern six-year-olds could explain the full process in detail, with graphic illustrations, printed from the internet! He came once a year, and Ma would be reminded to 'look out for the Cookstown Man' several times before Da departed for work. The byre would have to be 'dunged out' to operating theatre standards, and the poor oul' cow would be left tied up in it, often roaring her head off, ('lukin' away', as it was called), for most of the day. She would have to be watched like a hawk, and any 'fresh deposits' removed immediately from behind her, in case 'the place' would be disgraced. I saw a joke once, that the Queen must think the entire world smells of fresh paint, as everywhere she goes gets 'done up' for the visit - the 'Cookstown Man' must have thought that cows never dunged, if all the byres he was called upon to enter were as carefully looked after as ours was, at least for those few hours.

The 'Cookstown Man' would duly arrive in his car, in the obligatory Ministry Uniform of dark suit, collar and tie, and a hat. Da would have to be procured from his work, while the mysterious stranger opened the car boot, removed a large black bag, and changed into a pair of CLEAN wellies (unheard of in the farming community!) and a CLEAN brown coat, such as was worn by staff in hardware shops. Him and Da would disappear towards the byre, and some mysterious rites were obviously performed, as I was chased into the house by Ma, to 'stay outta the road' until it was all over. He reappeared a short time later, removed the coat (still CLEAN) and the wellies, (still even CLEANER) which he wiped on the grass before replacing them in the boot of the car, along with the black bag. That was IT. No explanation, no nothing!

Many years later, a friend of mine was working for the Ministry of Agriculture in South Armagh, where the same surnames abound, so everyone has a nickname, to distinguish between different branches of the same extended family. A son of a local 'Widow Woman' joined the Artificial Insemination branch of the Ministry, and a new nickname was born – his Ma was referred to exclusively as 'The Bull's Mother' from that day forward.

The clean wellies reminded me of another incident, where the vet had been called out to a small farm late one winter's evening, to examine a sow in labour. He arrived in his good suit, having come from some family function, put on his clean wellies from the boot of his nice clean car, and proceeded very carefully to look over the animal, avoiding contact with any 'offensive' material on the way. Job done, he took the totally unnecessary precaution of wiping his still-spotless wellies on the grass before returning to his car. In the dark, he did not notice that the farmer had been using a nearby gap in the hedge as a 'duncle', emptying wheelbarrows of pig manure through the gap, so that it slid down into the field, several feet below, for spreading at a later date. The still-spotless vet stepped too close to the edge, missed his footing on the grass, and followed the manure down through the hole, into several feet of moderately-liquid pig slurry! The farmer had some difficulty getting him out, and even greater difficulty not actually collapsing with laughter and falling in beside him.

'Drap' calves

The calf would be removed from the cow as soon as it was born, and reared separately in a pen of its own. In fact, Tom Dougan might arrive home from the next market with a 'drop calf' or two in the cart, to be reared along with it, as the cow produced enough milk for us and several of them. Buying drop calves was bit like buying a used car nowadays - the 'one careful owner' and 'little old lady who only used it for going to church' school of salesmanship was all too prevalent, and the calves often died like flies. A friend of mine tells the one about the farmer who bought two of them, and when someone enquired about them a month later, he was told, "One was OK - it died the next day. The other one lingered for a fortnight, and cost me a fortune in Vet's bills". I remember reading a story by Owen Kelly, I think, about the cattle dealer on his way home from the market with a few calves in the trailer, and stopped with a farmer he spotted along the roadside, hoping to 'off-load' a couple. The farmer eyed the sorry looking 'bastes' in the trailer, and replied "Ach, I'd have bought one, surely, but I left the spade in the moss", implying that it would cheaper in the long run to smack it behind the ear with a spade than to suffer the trouble and expense of trying to rear it up! Maybe it was good luck, or good judgement, or just selective memory on my part, but I don't remember any dying on us.

The next episode was then teaching the calves to drink, as their instinct was to suckle their mother, and they did not connect this strange white stuff in a bucket with milk, or food. The trick was to wet your finger with warm milk, and put it in the calf's mouth, and encourage it to suck. And, boy, could they suck! It felt like your hand was disappearing down the front end of a jet engine - I don't envy a cow, presenting a very tender part of her anatomy to one or two of those things several times a day. Once it got the idea that food was available from this 'teat', you moved the finger gradually down into the bucket, so that it's mouth was under the surface, and it began to realise that more grub was available in this strange round hard thingy. After a few days, they would come running the minute you entered the shed, and even when out in the open in later life, they could be called from the farthest reaches of the field by rattling a bucket at the gate. The one thing you wanted to avoid was getting too close above them, as calves often throw up their head when drinking. They do it when sucking the cow as well – Gawd'elp their poor mothers, getting that 'tender part of their anatomy' hit with a bulldozer on a regular basis. No matter how cuddly a small calf may look, it has a ridge of bone across the top of its head that will have you seeing more stars than the Hubble Telescope if it caught you between the eyes with it, and a 'dunt' on the chin would flatten you quicker than an uppercut from Mike Tyson!

A lot of kids these days would be worried about getting bitten, and would not put a hand near a large animal's mouth, but one of the most enduring memories of my childhood would be the roughness of a cow or calf's tongue, and the way the horse could lift sugar lumps off the palm of your hand with his lips, without touching you with his teeth.

Cows ancient and modern

This 'hands on' or even 'fingers in' approach meant that every 'baste' on the farm knew you personally, and were very familiar with people. You could walk right up to most of these animals in the open field when they were older, and they would often come to you when called. In later years, we had a bullock called Arnold (after a lad in my class at school) that used to let my sister ride on his back. These days, many calves of the beef cattle breeds are reared 'on the cow', and are almost wild animals in comparison. They often have very little human contact, and there are many more instances of cattle killing or injuring people as a result. People worry about being attacked by a bull - a herd of cows with suckling calves is far more dangerous. If a man or dog comes between a cow and her calf, she might take it as a threat, and attack, something that never happened when the calves were reared separately. Even the animals are bigger, and heavier, as a two-year old Charolais or Limousin bullock is a huge beast compared to the scrawny, half-starved two-year-old 'whiteheads' I would have known in the 1950s. Supplies of hay were harder to 'win', as almost a week of dry weather was needed to get a field cut, turned, dried and stacked, all of it by hand, so winter-feeding was often scarce, and buying meal too expensive. By the time spring grass was growing, many animals were thinner than Posh Spice on hunger strike. I remember an elderly neighbour passing a remark about a farmer up the road, not noted for over-feeding his stock: "Yer Man must be going to build a couple of bullocks – I see he has the frames out in the field".

I was often regaled with horror stories when I went to school, from town kids complaining about being 'chased by the bulls' when out in the country. Usually it was a herd of matronly old Friesians, displaying their inherent nosiness by investigating anyone entering their domain to ascertain their business. The 'townies' would run, whereupon the cows would run after them – if anyone had turned round and said 'Boo' the cows would have stopped dead, and high-tailed it for the hills. When I tried to point this out, I was often assured that 'Oh, No, No! They were definitely bulls, 'cos they all had horns'!

Butter making

Our wee red cow produced far too much milk for us to use up, so it was collected in big black and red crockery containers, called 'crocks', and when enough had accumulated, it was emptied into the churn. This was a wooden barrel, with a lid that could be screwed down tight, on a sort of axle, which sat on a four-legged frame. One end of the axle had a long handle, which was used to turn it, for what seemed hours, until the cream separated out from the milk. We all took a turn at the handle, until Ma decided that the job was done, and skimmed the solids off the top, to make into pats of butter. There were wooden paddles for patting it into shape, and a round wooden stamp for putting a nice pattern on the top. Some of it went to the Dougans, but we ate the most of it ourselves, especially brilliant with soda bread, or pancakes, made on the griddle, over the open fire.

Sisters

My sister Bridget died at the age of four, a tragedy from which I don't think my parents ever recovered. She had been complaining of stomach pains for a while, and the Doctor had been out several times, but put it down to tummy upsets, etc, and gave her the usual 'white bottle' that was the standard cure for anything intestinal at the time. After two weeks getting steadily worse, she was rushed into hospital with appendicitis. She came out of the operation very well, but got a secondary infection, and had to be opened up again – not an uncommon occurrence in those days. The shock of the second operation killed her, and, I think, a substantial part of my parents as well.

I was about five at the time, and can only remember her as a small item with brown curly hair, and a pink dress, but can recall nothing of her face, or mannerisms at all. I had a horror of getting my hair washed at this time, and she took great delight in reminding me when it was due to happen. Ma used to hold my head face down over the basin, and pour water over the hair to clear the soap out of it, so I felt like I was being drowned. It never occurred to her that the same result could be achieved face up, with the water going over the hair only, as they do in hair salons nowadays. Mind you, Ma would not have been a great frequenter of hair salons in the 1950s, so would not have had much opportunity of finding this out! My only memory of Bridget is of her voice shouting 'hair washing time' after me, as I disappeared round the doorpost, and tried to blend invisibly into the surrounding countryside.

However, miracles do happen, and another baby sister was born a few years later, when Ma was forty-seven years old, which was a much bigger shock in those days than it would be now. She was named Rosemary, (Rosie) and managed to survive all that Drummondmore, dogs, cows and me could throw at her, and thrive on it.

Our little red cow was showing her age by now, so a replacement was acquired - a huge half-wild blue-roan Ayrshire heifer, with horns a foot long, which was immediately named Rosie as well. The heifer was 'watched like a hawk' for days before she was due to calve, as it was her first, and Da came home each day at lunchtime to check her out, as well as in the mornings and evenings. She was showing no signs whatsoever at six pm, and I was sent down the field to bring her in for the night at about eight pm, and she had the calf lying beside her, born and bred and buttered all by herself! She was very difficult to milk - she would 'kick the stars out of the sky', and hoofed many a bucket of milk into the middle of next week before Da got her calmed down. However, the following year, she was totally different, and even Rosie (the sister) could have handled Rosie (the cow) with no problems. Da could go out into the field with a stool and a bucket, and sit down, calling "Chay, Chay, Chay", and the huge beast would just casually wander across, and stand there in the open to get milked. I don't know why it was "Chay, Chay, Chay" in particular, but everyone seemed to use that to call cows - possibly a throwback to the ancient Irish, or even earlier, but it seemed to work anyhow. As long as the cow knew what it meant, I suppose, it didn't really matter about us!

Civil engineering

My most time-consuming summer pastime was dam-building, and many happy hours were spent knee deep in the small stream that ran along the foot of the hill, about one hundred yards from the house. There was an old orchard in between, so I was totally isolated, but could still hear any 'come in for yer tay' gulders from Ma at the front door. The stream was about two feet wide, but up to six feet in places, with very little water in the summer, and the banks were about two feet deep, in a thick reddish clay soil.

I graduated from a few stones across the stream at a narrow point in my earliest attempts, to very substantial constructions several feet deep. I would cut a few posts from the hedge, get the sledgehammer, and drive them in across the bed, and then weave other branches between them, to provide strength. The front of this was then coated with stones and sods of earth, and the soil smeared into mud, to prevent leakage. Water flowing over the dam would soon wash away the looser soil I had built into it, but I soon learned to re-route the flow through the unbroken clay of the riverbank, which would not wash away easily, and the dam survived for ages. A few sticklebacks were caught, and numerous frogs, but the main purpose of the exercise was the actual building, and the satisfaction of getting an even larger dam than the year before - the floods each winter, of course, scoured the entire site clean of any trace of human activity. Rosie stepped out unto one of these dams, aged about 4, and slipped, feet first, off the edge, into waist deep, very cold, water. I don't know if it was mortal terror or an anti-gravity device that got her out, but I think she held the world record for acceleration in a vertical direction for several years, until beaten by Yuri Gagarin, and he had a little assistance from a rocket strapped to his rear end!

4 VISITORS

Doggy Men

Da used to be a member of the Beagle Club, and went off to annoy the local hare population most Saturday afternoons in the hunting season. I don't think they ever caught much, so it was more of a social occasion. Beagles have very short legs - people used to keep the huntsmen going about having to 'lift them over the puddles' on wet days - so their chances of catching double pneumonia were considerably higher than their chances of catching a hare. When the hunt was in our area, men used to drift into the yard, in ones and twos, with a dog or two attached to their arm by a loop of the inevitable baler twine. No jewel-encrusted collars, or fat belly-dragging lapdogs here - these were lean, fit looking hounds, with a look in their eye that suggested they knew that they had to perform on a weekly basis, or they'd be getting 'the sack'. And that usually meant an all-too-real hessian sack with a concrete block in it, and a free swimming lesson 'thrown in'!

The men were usually on the thin side as well - a lifetime of hard work and forty-Woodbine-a-day does not contribute to galloping obesity, and spending your weekends chasing after a pack of dogs would take care of any stray cellulite that managed to overcome the lifestyle. No 'jolly fine chaps in hunting-pink', or jodhpurs either - the 'natty gents outfitting' of choice appeared to be ancient, shiny dungarees, often with a torn pocket or two, and patches on the knees, an even older looking jacket, and a pair of wellies, or hob-nailed boots that probably weighed more than the average beagle. A few had 'waterproof coats', that might or might not live up to their name when the inevitable Irish weekend deluge came on, but most put their trust in the traditional flat cap, and the stern faith of the Ulster Farmer that 'sure a wee drap'o'rain never hurt anybody'. Carrying an umbrella would have been unthinkable!

One character I remember was called Billy Graham, and any resemblance to the famous Evangelist of the same name ended right there. He was a scrawny wee craythur, about five-foot-nothing, with huge thick 'Guinness bottle' glasses, and it was widely rumoured that the last time he was clean was when the midwife washed him. He always appeared in the full Doggyman's uniform of torn dungarees, filthy wellies, even filthier cap, and ancient jacket, and he was known to one and all as 'Sigmanree', for reasons I never understood. Many years later, I read a book about the Korean war, which was going on in the early 1950s, and saw a photo of the South Korean Leader, Dr Syngman Rhee. The face, the height, the weight, and the glasses were almost identical - he looked exactly like Billy might have done, after four or five trips through an industrial-strength car wash, a new suit, and a local anaesthetic to remove his cap. (a 'capodectomy', perhaps?)

Billy worked Saturday mornings in a neighbouring farm run by two old brothers, who had an elderly 'sarvint girl' of the 'not too bright, but good with heavy weights' variety, noted more for her Nora Batty stockings than for her personal hygiene. Farms at that time seemed to have an endless supply of middle-aged women of this description, usually from the West of Ireland, who 'lived in', with little or no pay, or time off, and very little chance of getting another job, so they were virtually domestic slaves. Billy often came across the fields to our house after dinnertime, before heading off to the hunt. Da heard that Billy was 'aisy turned' - i.e. made sick - so he told him about visiting the place, and seeing Oul' Martha making butter, with the lice dropping off her hair into the churn. Poor Sigmanree spent the next half hour out on the street, 'bokin' aff rings round him', in all directions. He was back almost every week, though, to be regaled with some other horrifying tale of culinary ineptitude, or hygienic criminality. Eventually he got that he wouldn't eat a bite in their house, and rushed away every Saturday at dinner time, pretending some urgent business, as his poor oul' guts heaved at the very thought of sitting down at their dinner table. To be fair, it might have got a few 'F' words out of Gordon Ramsay if he had seen it, but was nowhere near as bad as Da and the huntsmen painted it, for the oul' doll and the brothers who owned the place survived well into their old age. Maybe they were just resistant!

The 'Boys' of the hunt club, as Da called them - most of them were the wrong side of forty, or maybe even sixty - would gather up the dogs, all yelping with excitement, and head off across hedges, fences, lanes, and railways, through bushes and rushes, bogs and flax-holes, for an occasional glimpse of the pack streaming along behind a hare, or hear the distant 'hounds gowl' of a beagle in 'hot pursuit'. The hare never went too far from its home patch, so the hunt would generally circle round and come back. If you were of a patient nature, and found the right hill to stand on, you might reduce the effort involved to a mere dander. Every man was hoping his dog would be in front when they hove into view, and ours often was, for Da had little patience with an animal that was not up to the job.

One of our beagles won 'Best of Breed' at the Armagh County Show in the early 1950s, and the cup held pride of place on the mantelpiece for many a year, but in those days performance was far more important than appearance. He was a black and tan dog called 'Driver', but if he hadn't been doing the business, even marrying a doggy Posh Spice wouldn't have kept him in the team! I went with Da to a few of these episodes when I was young, but my heart was never in it. I remember one particular hunt, where the snow came on around lunchtime, and the show was abandoned when it became apparent that it was not kidding, and it was like a white-out on the Greenland Ice Cap before we struggled home. My wee legs were having trouble enough, so God help the beagles, (male or female) which must have had the tenderest parts of their anatomy dragging in the drifts! Ma was loud in condemnation, with dire warnings of 'gettin' the chile a founder', and other predictions of doom, but Da stoutly defended the traditional 'Ach, houl yer wheesht, Missus, sure a wee drap'o'snow never hurt anybody' viewpoint, and so it proved in the long run.

Even following the hounds was often a major feat of navigation, as many field boundaries were 'double hedges' - two rows of twenty-foot-high hawthorn, and maybe a three-foot ditch in between. A term 'ditch' was applied equally to a water-filled trench, or a built-up rampart, and a good hedge often featured both - a farm boundary was often a three-foot wide 'sheugh', with the soil thrown up into a ridge of equal size, and planted with hawthorn, with substantial ash trees every few yards. The resultant barrier would almost stop a tank. In fact, in World War Two, slightly larger hedgerows in the Normandy Bocage country actually DID greatly hamper the Allied tanks, in the D-Day campaign. And like Field Marshal Montgomery, if the average doggy-man found his advance was bogged down, he had to retreat, regroup, and renew the assault in a different place, so progress tended to be in a rather zigzag fashion. Local knowledge was a big advantage in matters like this, and I would have known the location of the 'navigable' holes in most of the hedges for several miles around our house, and could progress across country quite quickly, whereas a stranger would have to size up each field in isolation, and hope that they did not get stuck in too many dead ends.

Any holes in these hedges tended to be plugged with the cheapest 'stop-gap' available - a few substantial hawthorn branches might be whacked off a nearby bush with a 'slasher', or bill-hook, and shoved in, butt end first, with a pitchfork. In many cases, an old car door, or an old metal bedstead might be used, or any substantial-looking item that came to hand. Many a Ford Anglia or Morris Minor ended its life in a ditch, and there are probably a good few lying there still. Rare indeed was the farmer who would waste good money on new barbed wire, or any of that nonsense, when cheaper materials, held in place with a few loops of last year's baler twine, would do the job. Fencing cattle is often a matter of 'smoke and mirrors' – if it looks solid, they will probably not even make an attempt to break out, but once they know there is a hole somewhere, they will usually manage to 'bull' their way through it. The easy availability of wooden pallets these days has meant that most modern motors end their days in the scrap yards, but many of their predecessors went to their eternal reward in a much more rural 'rusting' place.

Card Men

Da was noted as a great card player, in an age when card playing was the greatest (and often only) amusement of almost everyone, and a card school used to meet in our house every three weeks. They played 'twenty-five', a complicated game with lots of mysterious rules about what card beats what, and lots of things that were 'not done' such as trying to maximise your own tricks, at the risk of allowing someone else to get the five tricks required to win. Playing 'partners' made it even worse, as you needed psychic powers to divine what your partner had in their hand, and how they were going to play it, and the entire table might explode if you did the wrong thing, such as beating a low man with a big card, when someone else was 'sitting twenty' and only needing one trick to win. It was only one old penny a game, and with eight or ten players, a shilling would last you all night, even if you lost every hand. Ma used to play, to make up the numbers, but was never as skilled as the experts, and seldom survived a night without an exasperated "Good God, Missus" from Da, at some obscure, but obviously unforgivable, error. (He never called her anything but 'Missus' in all the years they were married) I was far too young to play, but did learn one valuable lesson - I have been a confirmed non-smoker ever since. With eight or ten men on the Woodbine, Capstan, or Gallagher Greens and Blues, the cigarette smoke started off as a grey layer near the ceiling, and gradually thickened as the night wore on, until it got down to my level, at which point I could no longer see the far side of the room. There were no cork tips, either - everybody was inhaling enough tar to re-surface half a mile of motorway!

On the weeks in between, they used to meet in McCann's at Abbey Park, (where the new school is built now) and O'Callaghan's, at the Seminary Farm of St. Patrick's College. (the buildings beside the graveyard) Jimmy O'Callaghan used to be the ploughman in Armstrong's when Da worked there, and they remained firm friends until Jimmy moved to Scotland, in the 1950s. Twenty years later, I lived in Scotland for a while, and visited the O'Callaghans in Glasgow, with my own wife and kids, and played 'twenty-five' in their house again. Forty years later, I was working in Lurgan, with a young fellow from Scotland, whose next-door neighbour and best pal at school had been Jimmy O'Callaghan's grandson. As the man says, it's a small world, unless you have to walk across it!

Jimmy Murphy was another frequent player - he had a tinsmith shop in Lower English St, near the foot of Banbrook Hill. The shop was known as the 'land that time forgot', as it was piled to the roof with buckets, baths, metal receptacles of all kinds and descriptions, which had been left in for repair, that Jimmy never got round to doing. There was a narrow, winding path from the door to the little room at the back where he worked, and the 'heavy metal' was piled up to the roof on all sides. If you wanted something fixed, you had to stand over him till it was done, or it was added to the ever-increasing pile, to wait it's turn, which was always 'first thing tomorrow'. It was rumoured that there was a bucket near bottom of the pile that Noah had used to bail out the Ark. Jimmy's brother Mick used to play cards as well, and they often had 'animated discussions' over playing strategies after the game. Mick grabbed the Tilly lamp from the hook on the ceiling one night, and had to be forcibly restrained from chucking it at his brother, after a particularly frank exchange of views!

Another neighbour, John Vallely, used to play too - a tall, elderly man, who lived a couple of fields away, over the hill, and who was noted for his tall tales. He had worked in Scotland in his youth, and told us of having a bath after his shift down the coalmine, and the water was so thick with coal dust that you couldn't stir it with a stick when he was done. He claimed to have stood on the top of a mountain in Scotland with binoculars, and read the time on the clock on Armagh Cathedral. I worked out some years later that Scotland is North-East of here, and the clock on Armagh Cathedral faces South

– not that I would doubt the man's word, or anything! Tam from next door, the famous pipe-smoking match-waster, played as well, and several others came and went, but apart from the card men and the doggy men, we had few visitors.

Motorists

Tom Dougan, the farmer, was the father of Jack Dougan, who owned the chemist shop in Ogle St. Jack was one of the first people about the town to acquire his own car, and he used to come out some wet Sunday mornings to take us in to Mass in Armagh Cathedral. The car was a tiny black Austin Seven, but had the most fantastic sounding horn I've ever heard. It was just a trumpet-shaped thing, with a rubber bulb on the end that you squeezed by hand, and it made long flat "oooooooooogah" noise like a duck with a bad throat. He used to sound it when coming along the lane, to let us know he had arrived, and it was the height of my ambition to get a horn like that for several years. I wasn't bothered about the car - the horn would have been quite sufficient!

One of the few other cars that arrived in our street belonged to a workmate of Da's - he arrived in another tiny black matchbox, with several others. He left his sister, in her early teens, in the car, and went off with Da to look at dogs, or something. The handbrake, if such a thing existed, must have been off, as the car began to roll down the street, tipped off the cobbled area, and headed down the path towards the river, gathering speed all the time! Luckily, it failed to take the curve, and banged into an old tree before it got going too fast. The girl was shocked, but otherwise unhurt, and so was the car - they built them solid in those days!

Mannix Fox, son of Da's sister, used to come down from Warrenpoint, on his motorbike, and this was one of the highlights of the year. (An 'interesting' name - he had been born in 1920, while Archbishop Mannix, from Czechoslovakia, was visiting Armagh) He arrived with a roar that could be heard all the way along the lane, in a huge thick overcoat and helmet and goggles, with great big gloves that went halfway up his arm, like a man from another planet. He sometimes took me halfway out the lane on the back of the bike when he was going home, and I would walk back to the house. No matter what speed it was doing, it seemed lightning fast to a stone-age kid, who seldom saw a car, never mind a magical machine such as this.

Our other main visitor was Ma's older brother, Charlie Rooney, from Keady, a tiny, thin, sallow-skinned man, who sometimes made Sigmanree look well fed and prosperous. He always wore a flat cap, and almost as big an overcoat as Mannix, but definitely no motorbike to go with it. When he removed the coat, he seemed to disappear, as it constituted at least eighty percent of his overall volume. He used to bring us a small bar of Dairy Milk chocolate each, and then beg half of it back off us as we ate it! Her older brother, Mick, stayed with us for a while when he was fixing the thatch on the roof, but he rarely appeared apart from that.

Foreign Travel

If we had few visitors, we rarely had the chance to inflict ourselves on others either. With no car, we rarely left the house when I was young, as you can't take a family of four too far on the bar of a bike. There were a couple of day trips to Bangor, to visit Ma's former employers, the Miss Bleakleys, which involved a journey on the train, but was so long ago I can't remember much about it. We wandered up and down the prom, gawping at the famous 'Pickie Pool', and amazing sights like people actually swimming! We had no TV, of course, so such things were the stuff of legend, seen only in cartoon form, in the Beano. Naturally, we did not indulge in such avant-garde, Anti-Irish-activities!

Da's niece, Maureen Connolly, had to go into hospital to have a baby, so we got a week or two just outside Newry, 'minding house'. There were five kids, plus her mother, Mrs Fox, (Da's older sister Caroline) who was partly bedridden after a stroke. It was a great holiday for me, but hardly for Ma, who had to get her up, put her to bed, and feed and clean for the whole mob in between. I think we did get a run to Warrenpoint, but that was it.

The only other place was an annual visit to Keady, to Ma's home place, to see the uncles. They lived in a wee thatched cottage in even worse condition than ours, on a small rocky farm near Clea Lough. Charlie was the 'housekeeper' of the two, who did the cooking and the shopping, etc. Mick was the oldest of the family, and was a slightly larger, solider, 'ball of a man', who did casual work on farms all around Derrynoose and Keady. He used to take me for walks around the 'rocks', as they called the lower part of the farm – a wasteland of rough grass, rocky outcrops, and clumps of whins, where a few half-wild cattle roamed at will. I really loved these visits, seeing a different part of the world, and (to me anyway) a lot more interesting than the seaside!

5 BEING A GOSOON

My uncle, Mick Rooney, being a Keady man, usually referred to any lad with an age in single figures as a 'gosoon' – from the Irish Gaelic, I think, meaning 'small enough to smack round the lug with impunity'. He also called a woolly jumper a 'gansey', and so on. They speak a different language in 'them thar hills' - the change of accent and expressions between Armagh and Keady was very noticeable to me when the uncles came to visit us.

Bicycle art

I used to ride Da's bike down the street in front of the house sometimes, when he was not at work. It was a traditional big, heavy, man's bike, with a bar, so I could not get my leg over it, so I used to put one foot on the pedal, and push myself along with the other, like a scooter. This had certain drawbacks, as the balance and control of the bike was a lot more difficult, and the brakes were almost impossible to use effectively. I used to start off at the gate of the field, at the high end of the yard, with the pedal at the top of its stroke, and the first push down was enough to get me started. The entire trip was only about eighty yards, past the house, barn, stable and byre, into the haggard at the lower end, and most of the street was cobbled, so it was a very bumpy ride!

I got my leg caught between the chain and the sprocket wheel once, and it nipped a piece the size of a shilling out of my calf, which suspended operations for a while, but such trivialities were soon forgotten, and normal service was resumed as soon as the leg was useable again. The duncle, piled high with 'bovine waste products', was directly opposite the byre door, and was the scene of my next disaster. I was 'flying' down the cobbles when a hen ran out of the byre door, right into the front wheel. The bike stopped dead, and without its momentum to carry it on, immediately toppled over. I went over with it, face first into the dung heap, with my knees banging into the cobbles, and various other bits of me banging into the bike, or (so it seemed) any other available item of hardware in the vicinity! I staggered up the street to the door, covered in blood, dirt, and dung in equal measures, crying like a green faced baboon with its tail caught in a mangle. It took Ma a half hour to repair the damage - five minutes to clean me up, five minutes to wallop me for dirtying my clothes, and the first twenty minutes to stop laughing. I went back to the scene of the crime later, and there was a perfect imprint of my face in a soft part of the duncle, which lasted several days until washed away by the next rain. The hen - as the perpetrators of such mayhem so often do - escaped relatively undamaged!

Not-so-big game hunting

Being alone most of the time, I had to make my own amusements, and one of my frequent pastimes was hen hunting. As I said before, these wily and cunning beasts roamed the back yard, led by the 'Rooster from Hell', and many hours were devoted to trying to catch one, and foil their cunning plan to take over the universe. The best method was an apple box, turned upside down, with one end propped up with a stick. A long string was tied to the stick, and some corn was placed under the box. When an unsuspecting hen went in to eat the corn, the mighty hunter would yank the string, the box would fall, and if all went well, the hen would be trapped under it. A cunning plan, but one fraught with pitfalls, not least being that not even hens are that stupid all the time. Even the chuckie equivalent of the Dingle Family soon caught on that there is no such thing as a free lunch, especially one with strings attached. After a few successful hunts, the method had to be shelved for a week or two, until the hens had forgotten how it worked. The rooster himself was even caught a few times, proving that world domination is not as easy as it looks at first glance. Just as Hitler and Napoleon made the fatal mistake of attacking Russia, he was undone by the prospect of easy grub, and took a step too far!

In between, the odd bow-and-arrow hunt might be tried, but these were a disaster. The possibilities of a small boy, running flat out, with a homemade bow, firing a bent arrow, scoring a hit on a madly squawking hen zig-zagging across a bumpy yard covered with lots of things to trip over must be zillions to one. Certainly none of the dozens I fired came anywhere close! I did get a lot of skinned knees out of it, though, and the occasional 'near miss' on my old enemy, the rooster, when he tried to do the 'gunfighter's walk' up the yard towards me. No hens were actually harmed in the process, as any caught were soon released, somewhat traumatized, but otherwise unhurt, as we were farm kids at heart, and knew the value of a good layer. Cat hunting was even more unsuccessful, as the mere appearance with bow in hand resulted in the proposed victim high-tailing it for the hills, and never appearing again till nightfall. I never hunted the dogs, as they were the 'good guys' and definitely on our side, against 'El Roostero' and the Multifarious Forces of Evil.

Making the bows and arrows seemed to occupy a lot more time than hunting, as it usually involved a trip to Halligan's shrubbery, a wooded area about a half mile away across the fields, where hazel thickets abounded. The right branch had to be selected, stout and straight, with no knots or kinks, and a number of thinner ones for arrows. These were cut, or broken off, if I had forgot to 'borrow' Da's saw, (a thick-ear offence, at the very least, if caught) and were usually peeled of their bark before use. The ends were notched, and a string tied across them, and arrows prepared as well - these had to be split at the back, and have feathers inserted, and tied in with thread. For the real connoisseur, the point would be split as well, and a small piece of stone or slate put in for an arrowhead, 'cos that was how Crazy Horse did it at Custer's Last Stand. (Actually, many of the Indians had Springfield rifles, but I did not find that out until many years later!) The resulting arrow was nose heavy, badly balanced, usually bent, and utterly useless, but what the hell - making it was much more important that actually hitting something with it!

Somebody got me a dartboard once, with six of those small darts with plastic flights, and I immediately embarked on a crossbow-building phase. This resulted in a pretty heavy, but quite strong weapon, that was actually dangerous to something other than the user - it could bury a dart in the barn door to a depth of a quarter inch or more, from a range of five or six yards. It was a bit too heavy to aim at a moving target, and I did not really want to hurt anything anyway, so once again, the building of it was much more interesting than anything it was ever used for.

Of course, one of my duties was to check the hens at the end of the day, to make sure they were all in the henhouse, and close the door, in case the fox got in. They seemed to know I was not hunting them any more, and would sit quietly on the perch while I counted them. During the day, if I hove into view, looking armed and dangerous, or even whistling nonchalantly for that matter, they immediately high-tailed it for the hills, squawking like mad, but at night, they seemed to know that peace had broken out, and just ignored me. Maybe they were not as stupid as I thought they were!

At least they had the wit to get into the henhouse before dark. Our neighbour, Tam, told us that when he was younger, his ma had 12 white ducks, which were her pride and joy, and she was terrified of the fox getting them. It was his job to round them up every evening, but he could never get them to go into the house to be closed up. They drove him quacking mad - finding them, rounding them up, and chasing them round the yard to get them safely housed, night after night after night, till one night he finally flipped. When he eventually got them in, he caught each one in turn, took it to the chopping block, and chopped it's head off with an axe! He was greatly amused at how they ran round the yard for a while with no heads! His ma was not too well pleased, but all the neighbours dined on duck for a week!

6 FARMING

Haymaking

The highlight of every year was the haymaking, and it always seemed to be a good summer in the 1950s. The meadow below our house had strips belonging to several farmers, including Tom Dougan, Da's former employer Willie Armstrong, the two Oul Brothers that Billy Graham worked for, and a couple of others. Someone with a tractor and mowing machine cut the hay, and it had to lie for a day or two, depending on the weather, to dry. Each swathe was then rolled over, with a rake, or fork, to let the hay underneath dry as well. I had a cut-down pitchfork, and could turn hay at almost walking speed, along with the best of them. When dry, two or three swathes were raked into one, by hand, or if you were lucky, with a horse-drawn, or tractor-drawn implement. This was then pulled into lumps, and built into big stacks.

One of the 'experts', such as Da, would start off a round heap, with an almost hollow centre, sometimes with a bed of bushes underneath, to keep it off the soil, if the ground was very wet. When it was two or three feet high, the builder got on top, and rose up with it, as it progressed. From the age of eight or so, I had to do some of the building, tramping the forkfuls of hay into place, and ensuring that it was evenly distributed, The trick was to place each forkful round the outside in turn, and then one in the middle, to 'tie' the others in place. At about five feet high, the stack began to narrow, and the job became more 'interesting', as you had less and less room to stand, and the final forkful had to be positioned just right on the top, to shed the rain away from the centre of the stack. It was then tied down, with ropes, to prevent any accidents if the wind got up. The ropes were often home made, by taking some hay from the stack itself, and twisting it into a tight strand, using a 'Z' shaped implement, called (incredibly enough) a twister. Yes, whoever named that one must have had a wild imagination!

The men pitching the hay up to me had little consideration for my lack of years, or even more spectacular lack of height, so I was often buried in huge forkfuls, before struggling to the surface, and tramping them into place. Da was the worst of them, as he considered any fork with less than a hundredweight of hay on it a 'spoonful', and he would land them up to me with the words 'Put that under yer heel, young Rafferty', much to the amusement of the assembled company. (OK - so people were a lot more easily amused in those days!) This was considered character forming, much in the same way that 'a cold bath and jolly good trashing' were used in English Public Schools, to train the future rulers of the Empire. However, it did mean that I learned the trade very quickly, and don't remember any of the stacks falling down afterwards, which would have been a disgrace beyond endurance.

If the weather was not co-operating, the hay did not dry well enough to go into full stacks, and it might be built into smaller, looser stacks, or 'shigs', which were half the size of haystacks, and were not tramped. There was a universal dread of hay 'heating' in the shed, if it was put in damp. This meant that the entire shedful might start to ferment, and go musty, as the heat caused by the bacteria built up - spontaneous combustion of hay sheds was not unknown after a wet summer. Two or more of these 'shigs' might be knocked into one proper stack if the weather improved later. In really bad years, or if the haymaker was particularly paranoid, 'laps' might be used. These were formed by gathering up a big armful of hay, rolling it over the arm, and placing it on the ground, so that the upper surface would shed the rain, but allow the wind to blow through the rest of it. That was the theory, anyhow - in practice, however, if the weather stayed wet, it often ended up as a small forkful of black rotting vegetable matter! Some farmers had great faith in laps, but others regarded them as a waste of time, and they often ended up as 'dung heaps', only suitable for dumping. There was one particular field, a triangular area beside the old railway, near Mullinure lane, that was always watched, as local tradition had it that it was unlucky, and was more often lost than won. This may have been due to it being on a north-facing slope, behind the railway embankment, or the farmer being too careful and wasting too much time trying to get it perfect, but everybody wanted to get their hay stacked before the 'triangle field' was cut, as dire warnings went round the country "Get Yer hay in -

Davy's cut thon field" the minute it was started. It used to be something of an achievement to get your hay stacked before the 'Twelfth' holidays, but nowadays, with all the 'bag stuff' (artificial fertilizer) being used, most of it is done and dusted before the end of June!

Later on, however, the 20th century caught up with us again, and we progressed to baling the hay, which led to the acquisition of another trade - bale building. The bales were built into stacks of seven or nine in the field, and left for a few weeks to dry further. They were then hauled into the barn for the winter, built four or five high, like huge Lego bricks, on a trailer. The best part was that the load builder got to stay on top for the drive home, so the job was very popular with the younger generation! Everyone ended the summer with hands in raw flesh from hundreds of bale strings, but at my age, that was a small price to pay for riding home like a Lord on top of the load.

The other great tradition of the haymaking season was the 'tea in the field', which was delivered by a bevy of assorted females from the farm concerned, assisted by any others on the loose in the vicinity, or so it seemed. Just as neighbours gathered to make the hay, neighbours' wives and daughters gathered to 'make the tay', and many a romance (including, of course, my own parents!) was instigated at such gatherings. A long 'safari train' of women, carrying big wicker baskets containing bread and butter (often the famous Keady Loaf, cut thick enough to make doorsteps), soda farls (home made), wheaten bracks, scones and pancakes arrived, all the workers sat down in a circle. Huge teapots full of a thick brown liquid, almost strong enough to be walked on, were produced, and big mugs of it were doled out to all and sundry. Almost anybody remotely connected with the haymaking, and often more than a few unconnected passers-by, were fed to bursting point, and a place was often judged by the quality of its haymaking teas. I don't care how much you spend on a gourmet meal, or how prestigious the restaurant you go to, a tastier feed than tea in the hay meadow would be difficult to imagine.

Of course, there were exceptions - one elderly bachelor nearby was known for a certain reluctance to part with a shilling, and his two spinster sisters lived at home as well, and were reputed to have an even more murderous grip on a pound note than he had. It was widely believed that the sisters used to count the number of men at the haymaking, and bring out one slice of bread extra. Thus everybody took one slice each, and there was one left on the plate. Rough farmers or not, they were far too polite to take the last slice, when they knew all the others wanted it as well, and the hostess would say "Oh, nobody want anymore, then?" and whip the plate away before anyone objected.

Threshing

The other great event that attracted a crowd was of course the autumn threshing. We only grew 'corn' for one or two years, when I was quite young. This was actually oats, of course, rather than the ten-foot tall 'Indian Corn' (maize) of the American Mid-West. I was too small to take much part in the threshing, but ran about like a mad thing anyway, probably getting in the way a good deal. The thresher was a big Garvie Mill, powered by a massive Fordson Major tractor, with a long belt to drive it. The thresher had to be 'dug in', to ensure that it was level, and not going to move – a small hole was made for each wheel, of varying depth if it was on a slight slope. Another Fordson Major ran a big Jones baler, which a man forked the straw into, as it came out the back of the mill. Another man looked after the bags of grain, removing the full ones from the back end of the thresher, and replacing them with empties. There were several outlets, so when a bag was full, the man switched the flow to the next bag, pulled the bag out, tied the top, put it on the load beside him, and clipped on another bag. The grain was filling into the other sack while he was doing this, so unless the crop was very heavy, there was usually a fair amount of free time between full bags, to contemplate the meaning of life, and whether or not to have another Woodbine.

Three men were on top of the mill - one to feed the corn into it, and two to 'loose' the sheaves - i.e. cut the string around them - and place them same-way-round for him to lift easily. I did this job myself in later years, at different farms, amid dire warnings about safety - the young fellow who had been 'loosing' a couple of years before me had stumbled, and put his foot down into the roaring maw of the mill. The spinning blades that threshed the corn instantly amputated his lower leg. I tried to stay in a kneeling position, as far as possible, in spite of being buried in straw at times, and to keep my hands, or other appendages, as far from the hole as I could!

A man with a tractor and buckrake collected the stacks of corn from all round the field, and pushed them to the space in front of the mill, where two or three were waiting with pitchforks to throw the sheaves up to the top. In the days before tractors, this might be done with a horse-drawn 'paddy' - an 'L' shaped weapon with long metal spikes along the ground, and a vertical back. This was slid under the stack, and the horse pulled it along, with the stack on it, in much the same way as the tractor pushed the buckrake. There were usually a few rats that had taken up residence in the stacks, and who did not realise that a heavy price was about to be paid for the weeks of free food, and dry accommodation. As the stack was reduced to nothing, they used to make a mad run for freedom, and a few dogs were always about to chase them down - a good fox terrier could dispose of them in seconds. One snap to break the spine, a quick toss in the air, and off after the next one!

I remember Da told a story about being at a threshing, when he was a lad, around the time of the First World War. Men were in short supply, and a rather substantial farmer's wife was helping with the pitching, wearing one of the long heavy dresses that were the fashion at the time. A rat burst out of the stack, in mortal terror, with a dog after it, and took refuge in the closest dark hiding place it could see - it ran up her leg, INSIDE the skirt! The woman calmly took ONE hand off the fork, waited till the rat reached her thigh, where there was something solid behind it, and belted it with the heel of her fist. She then shook her leg to drop the now dead rat to the ground, and carried on pitching, as if she had just swatted a fly! Even Da, who was not easily impressed, was still in awe of that woman fifty years later, and I must admit, if it happened to me, I wouldn't need to hit the rat - the smell of soiled underpants would drive him out instantly!

7 BEING A CUB

If I had been born in Tyrone, I would have been a 'cub' by this time, as they do not have children west of the Blackwater river - their young are universally referred to as 'cubs' (male) or 'blades' (female). I remember being at an event in Dungannon, and was standing behind two men, obviously farmers from the suspicious stains on their wellies. I heard one say "See thon big fella thonder, fernenst thon motorbike? That's Wullie Henderson's cub. He must've grew another foot since the turn o' the year". I was thinking this must have made his poor mother's life a misery, buying shoes for him, when I realized that it referred to his height!

Football

As I rarely had a live opponent to play football with, I used to practice on the front street, kicking the ball up on the thatched roof, and letting it roll back down, to be skillfully trapped, perfectly controlled, and kicked back up again. Well, that was the theory anyhow, and how it looked in my eyes - it was a good job that 'Motty' and the TV cameras were not there, as I doubt if Alan

Hansen would have approved of my 'first touch', or any other touch for that matter. More time was spent retrieving the ball from the hedge after missing the return, or from the back yard after kicking it clean over the roof, than actually playing.

On one occasion, Da was sawing firewood in the corner of the street, when I mis-kicked, and broke a pane of glass in the front window. I heard the roar of anger, and high-tailed it up the lane, with bits of firewood flying after me! I did a couple of hundred yards in overdrive, before feeling safe enough to slow down, as Da would have been roughly the same shape as I am now, and so was better designed for the throwing events than the sprints. I hid out in an old beech tree till nearly dark, and escaped with a minor wallop and a severe caution, once he had cooled down. In fact, I think I broke almost every window in the house at some time, in a 'one-man football' career spanning eight years or so.

This proved to be an excellent indicator of future prospects - I tried out with several teams in later life, both Gaelic and Soccer, and usually got one game before being quietly dropped, as I combined the speed of a three-legged tortoise with the subtle ball skills of an epileptic bullock! We did have occasional visits from a couple of lads up the road a bit, or from town, and got a real game, sometimes with as much as two-a-side, if Rosie played as well. She was keen to take part in anything that was going, and if not quite fast enough, (at the age of four) to play at full back, she at least made an excellent goalpost.

Local feeding

We were a bit isolated, to say the least, so Ma could really only get in the shopping once a week, and had to make do in between. We had plenty of spuds, carrots, turnips and cabbage of course, grown on the farm, with bacon or sausages, if available, for dinner. Ma was adept at making soda bread, scones or pancakes on the griddle, over the open fire, and there was always porridge for anyone who wanted it, so we never went hungry. Good plain Irish grub, and no shortage of it, that was to prove the inspiration for my best ever poem (Foreign Feedin) many years later. Ma used to get 'store bought' bread most weekends, but it was usually the unsliced 'Keady Loaf'. If she did the cutting, with a huge long breadknife, it was fairly even, but if Da did the slicing, it was often as thick as a doorstep at one end, and a thin as a wafer at the other. The butter was plentiful, so it usually looked like it had been put on with a plastering trowel, and the jam was never in short supply either. One slice was almost a meal in itself, with a mug of tea so strong you could have stood the spoon up in it! Da used to drink buttermilk along with his dinner, but I never liked the taste of it, and preferred straight water.

He also had something called 'ale-plant', which grew in a big glass sweetie-jar on the window-sill. He filled the jar with water, and put in some 'stuff', which grew like mad, and 'flavoured' the water, turning it into something like Ginger Beer. He poured off a mug or two of it for a drink each day, and re-filled the jar, to continue the process. The 'stuff' was some kind of yeast, I think, that had to be fed with sugar and water to make it continue growing. I have never seen it since, or heard of anyone using it, but it was supposed to be the cat's pyjamas in the 1950s. According to Da, it would 'put hairs on your chest like shot leeks', and prevent everything from in-growing toe-nails to World War Three!

School

I started at Banbrook Hill School in Armagh at the age of six, a year or two after most of my class. Ma had been reading me comics and stuff before that, so I soon caught up. We got the Beano and the Dandy every week without fail, and Korky the Kat, Biffo the Bear, and Desperate Dan were all personal friends before I ever heard of Janet and John in the official school readers. I had to walk a mile or so from home to school, along the old disused railway line - Ma used to leave me half way, and the current maid from the Dougan household would walk out to meet me for the rest. I was usually 'taken over' by the Finnegans, twin sisters whose parents ran the pub near the station. They were almost the same age as me, but were more experienced 'townies', and they used to compete as to which one would take my hand up to the school. I can vaguely remember being totally bewildered by a playground full of kids, after living in almost solitary confinement in Drummondmore. I was, of course, the smallest in my class, and probably one of the smallest in the school, even though there were kids up to two years younger than me. Walking the railway lines each day meant that I wore a pair of heavy boots, and these were used for self-defence (and possibly attack) on more that one occasion! I used to walk down to Dougan's for lunch, and again after school, when the current maid would walk me out the old railway line until Ma appeared to pick me up.

From the age of about eight or so, I used to make the journey by myself, passing along the edge of the railway station, with shunting trains all over the place, and a big turntable in use, for turning the engines. Most of them were still steam engines – chuffing along with clouds of smoke pouring out of the chimney, and black-faced drivers and firemen on the footplate, wearing grimy blue overalls. Cheerful men, who always spoke or waved as they went past in their metal monsters, like the absolute Lords of Creation, proud of having the best job in the universe, and the envy of every lad in the country. Many times I had to step aside and watch a train pass within touching distance - Health and Safety would have twenty kinds of blue fit nowadays! There used to be a big goods yard, with storage sheds, and the yard would be full of lorries, and Hermann Wordie's carts queued up for loads, with big quiet horses contentedly munching on nosebags, and drivers in dungarees and heavy boots gathered in small groups, setting the world to rights through a haze of Woodbine smoke. It seemed an absolute hive of industry, no matter what time of the day you passed through.

Last train

It all came to an end in 1957, when the railway finally pulled out of Armagh. The last train was packed like a sardine can, and I remember standing in our yard in Drummondmore, looking across the fields at the Armagh-Portadown line, as it chugged away, with all the passengers hanging out the windows, singing and cheering. We were singing 'Last Train to San Fernando', a popular song at the time, and jumping about as well, watched only by a few bemused bullocks, and an even more puzzled beagle or two, who did not know what they were barking at, but were more than willing to give it all they'd got. There was still plenty of activity on the railway after that, lifting the rails, lifting the sleepers, etc, but it gradually died away, and Armagh's last claim to be a working city, with factories, jobs, etc, seemed to die with it.

Friends

One thing I did acquire at school was a friend, called Ollie Toal, who lived on Banbrook Hill, and who used to come out to stay with us in Drummondmore in the summer holidays, and some weekends as well. Although technically a 'townie', Ollie was even more of a Munchie than me, and kept goats on the railway lines in Armagh, and had a brown and white dog called Rory, which lived to an incredible age. We roamed the hills and woods with dogs, built dams across the sheughs, played Cowboys and Indians, or Japs and Marines (neither would be very politically correct these days!) around the hills, shooting each other full of enough imaginary lead to sink a battleship, and generally enjoyed total freedom. We built guiders (soap-box carts) from any set of pram wheels that could be begged, stole, or borrowed, and ran them down the street in front of the house, or even down the huge, grassy hill towards the river, to see who could get the closest to it without actually falling in.

We got an old bike, with no chain, and rode that down the hills as well, skimming ever closer to the riverbank. On one occasion, Ollie was driving, and I was sitting on the carrier on the back, when we crashed on the steepest part of the hill. My shin made contact with the sprocket wheel, and three of the teeth dug into me as deep as they could go. I dare not report this to Ma, as the resultant walloping would have exceeded the pain of the sore leg, so nature was left to take its course - I still have the scars!

Bigger game hunting

There was something in a book I saw once, about big game hunting in India, where they dug a massive pit and covered it in leaves, for some large and unsuspecting animal to fall into, on its way to the local water hole. The two of us spent a whole afternoon digging a two-foot square hole, two or three feet deep, in the back yard, in the middle of the path where Ma walked out to the washing line. We got it nicely covered in twigs and grass, and sauntered nonchalantly along the path several times each, duly falling into the hole, with loud cries of surprise, having totally failed to spot it, due to the amazingly brilliant camouflage. When Ma was coming out for the washing, we lay in hiding, ready to pounce and deliver the coup de grace, but to our immense surprise, and disappointment, she somehow managed to avoid the hole! We could never work out if it was the heaps of long grass lying on the path, the unobtrusive three-foot high pile of soil lying alongside, or the fact that we had been digging and falling into the hole all afternoon (just outside the back window) that gave the game away, but we did not discount the possibility that Ma had X-ray vision, and may even have been Superman in disguise. Not only that, but she made us fill the hole in 'before somebody fell into it' - obviously, (being a woman, I suppose) she was not familiar with the basic concept of big game hunting.

Rawhide

As the only handy lads in the vicinity, we were often called upon as 'trail-drovers' and soon became the Gil Favour and Rowdy Yates (remember them fellas, do ye?) of the Drummondmore area. Many farmers nowadays have a trailer to move cattle from one area to another, but this would have been unheard of in the 1950s, where a dozen or more bullocks might be driven along the roads for miles between different fields, or outlying farms. The farmer, or 'Trail Boss' would usually bring up the rear, with a 'trail crew' of two or more boys to run ahead and close gates, stand in gaps, stop traffic, etc., along the way.

The cattle had to be kept moving at a brisk pace, so that they had no time to see weak places in hedges, or study alternative options, but would take the line of least resistance - i.e. the one we had pointed them in. If they were run too hard, or frightened in any way, they might stampede, and take off over the nearest hedge, like the Grand National field over Beecher's Brook. A dozen scrawny bullocks stampeding down a lane is hardly the same as a Texas Trail herd of three thousand streaming across the prairie, but if they broke into a field with other cattle in it, you had a hell of a time getting them separated out again. Of course, all the cattle you passed in the fields alongside the road, being equally nosey sods, came over to the hedges, and roared at them, which only made the need to keep moving all the greater.

They were usually easy enough to handle, but most were not used to traffic, and all you needed was one impatient motorist honking the horn at the wrong time, or revving the engine when going past, and your whole afternoon could disappear trying to undo the damage! The trick was to always have at least one boy in front, and usually two, so that one could stand in any openings and direct the herd past. This one had then to overtake the herd again, so the front man usually slowed the pace when they came to a well fenced bit, and the other one sneaked past as softly as possible, so as to not upset the beef. Certain known 'danger spots' were usually mentioned in the mission briefing, so the crew were prepared for a pre-emptive strike. Dodgy hedges, wide gateways, etc, might be listed, and most importantly, the location of any 'crochety oul buggers' who might take particular umbrage at finding several hundredweight of beef playing tig on their lawn. Particular care had to be taken to ensure that such places were protected, even at the cost of the cowboy's life, if necessary!

The payment for these trips was usually minimal, and a bag of chips was considered an executive bonus in the trade. For us, it was a day out, a change of scenery, and sometimes a bit of excitement thrown in, and a few bob in the hand at the end was an unexpected bonus.

Fashion consciousness

On one occasion, Jimmy Armstrong, son of Da's former employer, came for us to move cattle, and Ma, for whatever reason mothers do these things, (presumably to create a good impression) insisted I wear my good school trousers. (He was a farmer, fer Gawd's sake – if I had worn a pink kilt with matching accessories he MIGHT have noticed, but I doubt it!) We went off to South Armagh, to another farm, and shifted various mobile hamburgers between various locations, and I managed to stay relatively clean-ish throughout the entire operation. But (there is inevitably a BUT, is there not?) on the way home from Armstrong's, across the fields, we had to jump over a small river. However, it had just been cleaned out, with a digger, and was twice the width it was the last time we had gone that way. Ollie, of course, jumped it with ease, but my foot slipped in from the far bank, and went into the muddy water up to the knees or more. Needless to say, no form of defence was acceptable - he had managed to get home dry, so why couldn't I do the same? The fact that he was not raising a rude finger to the Gods of Fate, Destiny, and Cow Manure, by wearing his best clothes, was not considered! It was obviously a fiendish plot on my part to 'destroy the only dacent pair of trousers I possessed', and any appeals to common sense fell on deaf ears.

Ma used to go to town on a Saturday, to get the week's shopping, and one week Da spotted something we needed after she left, and sent Ollie and me into town to get it. We walked to town along the railway, but came back out on the same bus as Ma. Da, of course, being not only a man, but also a farmer, totally lacked the 'respectability gene', so it was 'come as you are' - i.e. welly boots, old jeans with holes, even older jumpers with even more holes, hair not combed, hands (and wellies) covered in Gawd-knows-what from Gawd-knows-where. Ma was HORRIFIED when she saw us at the bus stop in town, and we were hissed at to stay away, and pretend we did not know her! We sneaked into the back of the bus, and she sat near the front, talking to a 'fraightfully naice' well-to-do (well, considerably better-to-do than us, anyway!) lady from up the road. It all went well until we had to get off, all at the same stop, when the lady gazed at us in a rather puzzled fashion, saying, "Isn't that your little boy, Mrs Rafferty?" Ma was disgraced, and the walk down the lane was distinctly chilly, but nothing to the Nuclear Winter that descended on Da when she got home. His response was the standard male "Why? What's wrong with them?" - genuinely baffled at the supposed need for clean clothes to go to town in.

I'm afraid I have inherited his fashion sense, completely undiluted by the passage of years, and have been 'spoken to' rather sharply by disgraced offspring for appearing with inappropriate attire on more than one occasion. Some of my grandchildren are so 'cool' that they refuse to be seen in my car, never mind in my company!

Goat napping

Ollie kept a couple of goats tethered on the old railway banks near Armagh, and used to go morning and evening to milk them, and move them to a new feeding area. We acquired a couple of kids from these, a male and a female, which had the run of the grazing fields near the house, and eventually grew up to give milk as well. However, they were capable of breaking through any fence in the country, so the half-door had to be kept firmly closed, as they loved to get into the hall, and eat the wallpaper! They would nibble the bottom of the wall till a tiny bit came loose, and pull this, ripping a long strip half way up the wall, and be standing in the hall, nonchalantly chewing it when Ma burst out though the inner door, swearing like the proverbial trooper, when she heard the noise.

The male grew into a huge, smelly Billy goat, with horns two feet long, who would undoubtedly have tackled a lion, had one the temerity to appear in front of him. He soon considered himself Lord of the Manor, even more so than the Rooster-From-Hell had done. (He had departed to the Great Hen Coop in the Sky, by this time, where he was no doubt conspiring with Hitler and Genghis Khan to further his dreams of World Domination) The goat, however, had the power to enforce his opinion, especially intimidating Rosie, who was too small to fight back. If you met him on the street, he would stare at you with his head to one side, nodding occasionally to draw attention to his massive horns, and refusing to give way, unless charged at by a mighty warrior armed with Ireland's traditional weapon - the Ash Plant.

Readily cut from any Irish hedge, thick as your thumb for heavy cattle driving, or thin and whippy for chastising the legs of small boys, the ash plant was the universal weapon of my youth, and any farmer without one in his hand felt as naked as Wyatt Earp without his trusty Colt 45. Never mind all that 'Cuchulain with his sword and spear' nonsense - the ash plant was the 'Weapon That Won the West'!

A neighbour of ours knew a farmer in South Armagh, who had a prize herd of Friesian cows, of which he was inordinately proud, and which were kept spotless, and looked after better than his children. He took our huge, hairy, stinking, billy goat away in a trailer, and put him in the field with Yer Man's prize cows! The owner went mental, much to the amusement of his neighbours, who had been warned what to look out for, but he never found out who was to blame, so I am mentioning no names.

8 TOWARDS CIVILIZATION

Reading the carpets

When Ma washed the kitchen floor, she always put down newspapers, to keep us off it till it dried. There was a 'railway' of double pages from the Irish News laid from the front door to the back table, with branch lines running towards the fireplace, and the bedroom door, that we had to walk on, on pain of death. It was a broadsheet in those days, of course - not the tabloid version of today - so three double pages would have covered half an acre. This was great, as I would always spot an interesting headline or two as I walked over them, and was often found hunkered down, or even kneeling, reading the floor covering. Ma used to 'give out at me', that it had been in the house for a week, and I had never looked at it, but somehow the news never seemed to interest me until it was underfoot! The other place for catching up on World Events was, of course, the 'Little Shack Out Back', as the Irish News was also our main source of bog roll. Many a time I staggered out with numb legs and a 'ring of no confidence' around the nether regions after finding a really good article, and sitting too long on the wooden bench reading all the gory details.

The dark side

Our main route to town was the old railway, which ran in an almost straight line from near our house to the north end of Armagh. It was also a great place to play, as the embankments and the sides of the cuttings were covered in bushes, and provided some great hiding places, ideal for Cowboys and Indians, or war games. Most of it was used as rough grazing by a local farmer, so it had lots of cattle trails winding around the bushes, and the occasional 'cow clap' lying in wait for the carelessly placed size-nine. I remember one year that I walked in to Midnight Mass one Christmas Eve, and walked home alone out the railway banks afterwards. Anything to avoid having to leave the house on Christmas morning, but once again, something that would be totally unthinkable nowadays – I must have been about twelve years old at the time.

The night was almost moonless, and the walk totally terrifying, as huge bushes loomed up suddenly out of the darkness, and every rustle of a small animal, or hoot of an owl, seemed loud enough to wake the dead. I would have regarded myself, even at that age, as 'far too sensible' to believe in ghosts, and I was well aware that the biggest wild animal in the country was a fox, but knowing that in the stark light of day is one thing, and convincing yourself of it at two in the morning on a dark and breezy night, with the wind sighing through the bushes all around is a different kettle of fish altogether! What I did not know, however, was that some of the cattle were lying on the main pathway, and

I practically walked right into one. If the rustle of small animals in the undergrowth was scary, then a loud snort, and half-a-ton of beef suddenly materialising out of the ground at your feet, was decidedly trouser-filling! I can still remember the sudden feeling of cardiac arrest, and the utter relief when I realised what it was. However, I got home OK, with the shoes and the underpants un-sullied, and have never been worried about the dark sinc.

Civilization

The house had been thatched twice in the time we lived there, once in the early years, and my Uncle Mick Rooney did some repairs later on. However, it was not a good job, and the leaks were getting worse, so eventually we had to leave Drummondmore. In 1960, we got a wee house at Annacramp, on the Armagh-Loughgall road, in the same townland as the cottage where Da had lived with the Foxs forty years previously. He knew most of the neighbours, and we settled in very well, but such unknown marvels as electric light, running water in the house, and real people within a hound's-gowl, took some getting used to. Ma got a job the apple peeling with Gordon Scott next door, and we all helped out after school.

We even got a TV, and Da used to watch the football and boxing, and Ma learned to shout insults at Mick McManus and Steve Logan on the wrestling on a Saturday afternoon. She just did not seem to understand that the Ref deliberately kept his back turned, when telling off Steve Logan, so that McManus could wreck mayhem on his tag-team opponent, and was constantly surprised at the way the terribly battered 'good guys' always seemed to recover, almost miraculously, at the end, and win the match. I preferred the Tellygoons - a truly marvellous puppet show, using the scripts of the Goon show from the 1950s Radio series. I can still remember Neddy Seagoon and Bluebottle digging the Great Aircraft Canal across Africa, with a wonderful machine that could do the work of two men, and it only took three men to operate it!

Sadly, Da took ill soon afterwards, and died in 1965, in Armagh City Hospital, aged only sixty-one, a victim of too much hard work, and too many Woodbines - he had been smoking forty-a-day or more from the age of eight. Ma survived until 1988, (her 80th year) spending her last few years in a wheelchair, after breaking her hip. I lived in Scotland, England, and Wales, before moving back to Craigavon, and eventually to Loughgall. I worked in the Goodyear factory until it closed in 1983, and then re-trained as a computer programmer. Nowadays, I try to tell computers what to do, which is a lot safer than telling half-ton bullocks what to do, but somehow the level of bullshit generated seems even greater! I have somehow acquired a wife, three kids, and ten grandchildren along the way, something that still astonishes me from time to time when I think about it.

However, I have never forgotten my early years in Drummondmore, and how lucky I was to have a whole world virtually to myself when I was growing up.

9 POEMS

I used to write an 'odd ode' or two for the Goodyear Union Newsletter each month when I worked in the factory, (1976-1983) but I really never followed it up. It was not until I heard about the 'Bard of Armagh' contest in the late 1990s, and sent in a poem, based on Rev Marshall's 'Me'n'M'Da', ('Livin in Drumlister'). It was turned down, quite rightly, for it was pretty poor! I actually got tickets for the contest a year or two later, when it was held in the Moy Inn. It was won by Pat McGeeney that year, with 'Half A Bed To Let', still my personal favourite of all his poems. Patsy O'Hagan was second, with the 'New Generation', which I also loved, and I was totally gobsmacked with the brilliance of these guys, and all the others - ordinary people, who could do an extraordinary job at entertaining their neighbours.

I could not get a ticket the following year, so I decided the only way I could get in was to take part myself! I began re-writing my poem, to make it longer, stronger, and a lot funnier - the result was 'Divil The Wan Wud Hev Me', based on the idea that farmers meet a lot more women these days, but most of them do not want to be farmer's wives.

Farmers also tend to be more practical than romantic – Da (who was hardly Rudolph Valentino himself) used to talk about the fellow who proposed to his sweetheart (after a 10-year courtship) with the unforgettable words, 'Mary Anne, wud ye like till get buried with our ones?'

He might understand this guy!

Divil The One Wud Hev Me (2001)

I'm livin' all m'lone now, since m' Ma and Da passed on,
Just me an' Shep beside the fire – Ach, now the nights is long.
M'Da said till get a wumman, for a man shouldn't live alone
And it's bloody hard till drench a cow, when yer working on yer own.
A dacent, strappin' lassie, with lots o' charm an' grace,
Who could mebbe drive a tractor, an' help out round the place.
I went with dozens in m'time – God knows, Ah tried m'best,
But divil the one wud hev me, for the first one till the last

---

The first one that I went with was wee Bridget McAloon
She wanted flowers and romance, just like Mills an' Boon
Now I didn't have a motor then, so I really had no chance
For a Massey Ferguson 35 is not great for romance.
I hosed it down before each date, to clean off the cowshit,
And put a bale o' hay in the link box, to give her a place to sit.
But I lost her till a Fancy Dan, from somewhere near Glenanne,
With an Elvis Presley haircut and a Morris Minor van

The next one wuz totally different – from a solid farming breed,
When I seen the wellie marks I knowed she wuz the girl I need!
A body that would break the sweat on any farmer's brow,
A fist like a 10-pound hammer – and an arse like a Charolais cow!
She asked me home to meet her da – I thought, I'm in like Flynn,
But the oul' hoor only wanted help to fill his grant form in!
She could milk, or drive a tractor, as well as any man,
But she married a bloke from Portydown, with a bigger farm o'lan'

It wuz run me here, or take me there, or let's go till a show
Dancin' till the wee small hours, dressed up in fancy duds
The bags I had below me eyes wudda held a bing o' spuds !
Every night that we went out, we'd end up havin' rows,
'Cos I had trouble getting' home in time to milk the cows!
She thought me awful boring, and tied down till the land
So I got the push, and she tuk up with a drummer in a band

The next one wuz liberated – Just to watch her wuz a treat
She'd a chest like a pair o' wee lads, fightin' under a sheet !
She tried to educate me, to see the world beyond my work,
For there's more to life than slurry tanks, and how to smuggle pork !
She gimme plays, an' symphonies, and books as thick as thon,
By Russian blokes with names that ye could twist yer tonsils on !
When she mentioned Dostoyevsky, my big mistake I made
Sez I 'Wuz it him that useta play left-half for Partizan Belgrade'?

Then there was one I wrote till, from an ad in the 'Farming Year'
Single R.C. Female, seeks man with a big 'John Deere'
She showed me round the place she had, down beyont

Kildare,
'300 acres this side of the road, and 200 more over there!'
Sez she 'To plough a furrow up that long field can take 2 hours to do'
Sez I, 'I know jist what ye mean, I've a tractor like that too!'
But she said we wuz incompatible, of a totally different ilk,
For she was mainly arable, and I was pigs and milk.

Then I thought it wuz the place - ach, now, the house wuz rough
And weemin want electric, and washin' machines, and stuff.
So I done 'er up, from top till toe, with everything ye'd want,
And I made a lock o' shillin's, when ye counted in the grant!
The next one now, wuz right impressed, but still she turned me down
She said it was too quiet, an' too far out of town.
She wuz used till a more busy place, where life is fast and loose,
An' I could well believe it, for she come from Derrynoose!

The next wuz big Patricia - or wuz it Mary Jane?
Ach, the names run intil other, but the story's just the same
One thought I wasted money - one thought that I was 'tight',
No matter what the hell I done, I couldn't get it right!
One said that I was rather small, which I did somewhat resent,
Sez I 'I'm nearly five foot one' - but it wasn't that she meant!
They got older, and got plainer, as the years went past,
But divil the one would hev me, from the first one till the last

---

I tell a lie – there was the one, who might've married me,
But her ma had a mouth like a bucket – aff a bloody JCB!
Sez she 'Ma can live with us, and help out when the kids are young'
Sez I 'I'd sooner shovel suite, with a spoon tied till m'tongue!'
So I settled down till live m'lone, and work the place m'self
And ignore the sly and smart remarks, about bein' on the shelf

You'd think I'd one foot in the grave, though I'm only forty nine
An' I'm still a tight enough wee man, an' not long past m'prime!

The relatives keeps callin' round, like vultures round the bones
There's nephews an' cousins crawlin' out from under stones
It's 'How're ye doin, Uncle Mick,", and' 'Man, yer lookin' grand'
Divil the hair they care y'know - they only want the land!
When I mentioned a wee holiday, there wuz bloody near a fight
Over who was going to milk the cows, and keep the oul' place right
If they only knew the half of it, they'd have a flamin' fit
For I'm off to Lisdoonvarna - I'll get a wumman yit !

The first year I entered the contest, I was utterly terrified. I used to have a bad stammer when I was at school, and still suffer from it in moments of stress, so the prospect of standing up in front of hundreds of people and trying to make them laugh was indeed a daunting prospect. I knew that if I lost my place in the poem, I would never get it back, and descend into a total disaster. I find it easier to read things out, so I printed the poem out in large type, and kept it in front of me throughout the performance, so if I felt a nerve or two, I could look down, and read the next line, to get me over the crisis. As I was waiting to go on, I was thinking 'Never Again'! I did not have another idea in my head anyway, and I just wanted to get it over with, and sneak out quietly, never to return!

BUT - I actually got a few laughs!

I came in a reasonably respectable fifth, a long way behind McGeeney and O'Hagan, but still in there somewhere! (And a fella called Liam McNally, with a poem called 'Catched on the Broo', that I really laughed at!) And by the time I drove home, I had 2 ideas for next year . . .

One of them was based on an old story my Da used to tell, about a girl who got a lot of big ideas, and some of the local comics took her down a peg or two, with the aid of a goat.

Getting Your Goat (2002)

I'm a man that likes a quiet life, with the odd we bit o' craic,
I live with my daughter's family, in a wee room round the back.
They moved in when the Missus died – they said to 'keep me right',
But the only thing they're good for is converting spuds to . . . manure!
Her eldest girl was a tight wee blade, who never missed a trick,
With a temper like a nest of wasps you're poking with a stick.
Every stitch that she put on had to be the height of fashion,
Specifically designed, it seemed, to raise a young man's passion.
She'd go out in tiny miniskirts, in the wildest winter weeks,
The wind – it must have surely brought the colour to her cheeks!

But when she went away to Queen's, her head begun to swell,
And then she got a boyfriend, and things really went to hell.
It was lucky that astronomy was not her chosen class,
For she had the clear impression that the sun shone from his ass!
His suits were by Armani, and his shirts were silken fine,
His shoes were all Italian, and his drawers were Calvin Klein.
His name, it seemed, was Jeremy, he lived out in Cultra,
He was just like Daniel O'Donnell, only nicer to his Ma!
She reckoned he was perfect, but I didn't know what to think,
For he sounded like a fella who might like his handbags pink!

Then one weekend she landed in, just like a nuclear bomb,
He was coming down next Friday, to meet her Dad and Mum!
The house had to be whitewashed, and paint work all re-done,
And the yard cleaned up and tidied, and wash off the cow-dung.

The floor was scrubbed, the brass was rubbed, the dog was booted out,
But then she dropped a bombshell that made me want to shout.
She wanted my wee sitting room, with a sofa and TV,
Where she could take her darling Jeremy, to sit down after tea!
In vain I tried to protest, but I didn't want a row,
But I went down to the byre, and complained like Hell to the cow!
They tidied and they painted, dusted, cleaned, and swept it all,
Till the house felt like a convent, when the Pope was due to call.

When the great day came, he left Belfast, in his lovely new sports car,
And got on great until he reached the lanes of South Armagh.
There's not much satisfaction having hundreds of horsepower,
When you're stuck behind a tractor, doing twenty miles an hour.
And when the tractor finally left, his speed slowed to a crawl,
Behind a herd of cows that filled the lane from wall to wall.
Now boys brought up in nice Cultra have a lovely view of cattle,
Clean and smiling things in books, that give milk in a bottle.
But folk reared in the countryside would know this is not right,
For a Friesian's life's ambition is converting grass to . . . fertilizer!

And though they live all day in fields, with room to drop their load,
They always seem to save it up, and carpet-bomb the road!
Now Yer Man got up a bit too close to this lovely rural scene,
And the whole front of his lovely car got painted brown and green.

A COUNTRY GLIPE

And when he wound his window down, a loud complaint to make,
He got some more 'collateral damage', right across the bake!
So all in all, the tea we had was a somewhat strained affair,
For Jeremy just moaned and groaned about his lovely car.
The countryside was beautiful – each field a perfect scene,
But those farming chappies really ought to try and keep it clean!
They've reared these blasted animals from calf to milking cow,
Yet they defecate upon the road – they should be trained by now!

When the awful meal was over, I went out for a walk,
For I'm not the greatest in the world at making fancy talk.
I got back near the edge of dark, it must've been half eight,
When I spied her brother Michael, leaning sadly on the gate.
'How's the big romance?' says I, and he answered, somewhat loth,
"If she marries thon big asshole, we'll be scundered with them both!"
Now this lad was a skinhead, and he had less brains than hair,
And more ear tags than a bullock on its way to Newtown fair.
But at that moment we agreed, two minds with but one theme,
When a sudden notion struck me – a really lovely scheme!
Says I "I've got a cunning plan, that might just work, with luck"
"D'ye think could you give me a hand to catch oul' Paddy's Buck?"

Now Paddy was a neighbour man, with goats that roamed at will,
And the leader of this wandering band was a big old smelly bill
You knew when he was coming, for his smell went on ahead,
Like a cross between a pig farm and a rat that's three weeks dead.

He terrorized the countryside, men and women, dogs and sheep,
He was used to threaten children who wouldn't go to sleep!
He had butted seven women, two policemen, and a car,
Plus five Marine Commandos, and fourteen UDR!
He would tackle any living thing that ever had been born,
He even gave Parish Priest a good dose of the horn!

Me and him got on the best – we had a non-aggression pact.
He knew I had walking stick, and his arse had once been whacked!
So Michael went and gathered up some nice sweet grass to use
To make the goat an offer that he just could not refuse!
We led him softly up the yard, and we slid the window wide,
And made sure he was watching, as we placed the grass inside.
Peace had broken out, it seemed, inside the little room,
The trials of the day forgot, and love once more in bloom.
Tea and buns had just been brought, and a brand new biscuit tin,
When a wee breeze stirred the curtains, and something wafted in.

As Jeremy raised cup to lip, his hand in mid-air froze,
As a strange and foul aroma assailed his cultured nose.
And when he moved the curtain, to investigate the smell,
He found himself six inches from a face straight out of hell!
His scream was long and piercing, and he jumped up three feet high,
The cup of tea that he had held went flying through the sky!
And of course, as luck would have it, young Mary bore the brunt,
For the contents of the cup of tea all landed down her front.
Them wonderbras they tell me, heads 'em out, and rounds 'em up,
But when it comes to scalding liquid, they'd hold damn near half a cup!

Now I've read of saintly women, who bore pain in silent prayer,
But to cross your heart with burning tea was more than she could bear.
She yelled, and jumped, and capered, in a wild and screaming spin,
While tearing at the roasting cloth that was glued unto her skin!
She called yer man a list of names, in language far from nice,
She was not a girl for one cross word, when a dozen would suffice!
The noise brought mother through the door, going hell for leather,
She saw the torn and shredded blouse, and put two and two together!
A couple of my old walking sticks were standing in a rack,
And in a thrice she grabbed one, and whacked him o'er the back!
He tried to run towards the door, but the women blocked his way,
He ducked and dived this way and that, like a cornered rat at bay.
In vain he tried to protest, but the words stuck in his throat,
So he dived out through the window, and he landed on the goat!

Now the goat had got an awful shock, when yer man yelled in his face,
His horns had caught the curtains, and they held him fast in place.
He was struggling still to break the grip, when the boyo hit him hard,
So he ripped them right out of the wall, and buck-lepped up the yard.
Yer man hung on with tooth and claw, like a monstrous carbuncle,
But the jockey was unseated, just they cleared the 'duncle'!
At least the landing ground was soft, with squelchy bits in places,

It's amazing just how well the stuff can stick to suits - and faces!
He struggled up, and staggered out – one shoe left in the glar,
And in 3 buck-leps he crossed the yard, and squelched into the car!

He roared away like a superstar from a Rally Driving class,
And down the lane like the Hounds of Hell were snapping at his ass!
Michael sneaked back to his room, and I didn't come home till ten,
And asked if Jeremy had gone - full of innocent concern!
I was informed, through gritted teeth, that he had not been well,
And gathered that he might be back, on the first cold day in Hell!
The best-laid plans o' mice and men, gang aft aglae, it seems,
But our plan had come together, beyond our wildest dreams!

As described in this book, I was raised on a very primitive small farm, with no electricity or water supply, run much the way it would have been in the 1800s. In fact, the BBC program 'Victorian Farm' brings back a lot of memories for me, as I have seen most of those techniques and implements in my youth. I am now working as a computer programmer, so I have often thought that I have seen about 200 years of progress in one lifetime. Then I saw an article about a tractor with a GPS that could go out and plough a field all by itself, and this was the result! I thought I was doing well with this one, but a tall, elderly, distinguished-looking gentleman called Henry McGrath turned up, looking like butter wouldn't melt in his mouth, and produced a classic poem about his operation in 'Daisy Hill', which won it by a mile!

The Uncommon Agricultural Policy (2003)

The farming isn't paying much, in these ultra modern days
With the price o' pork, and the C.A.P., and the fut'n'mouth disease,
I was thinking hard of quitting, and signing on the broo,
But shovelling' dung, and smuggling' pigs is all that I can do!
So when I heard the rumours, sure I phoned up right away,
And a boyo from the Ministry, landed out the very next day.
Says he, we're looking for a place that's sad and badly run,
To try a new experiment our chaps are working on.
We can install computers, and connect your beef and mutton,
You'd be able for to run the place at the touch of one wee button.
It would feed your pigs, and bullocks, and run your milking plant!
Says I, My only question would be – will I get a grant?

The EEC would pay for all, and so I signed the chit,
And soon the place was ankle deep in wires and bullock shit.
I offered to clean up the yard, but the boyos didn't mind,
They said their job was ankle deep in bullshit all the time!
There were hardware men & software men, and all they did was talk,
And each one blamed the other, if something did not work.
The bloke who wired the calf house – he got a wee bit stroppy –
He complained that our wee heifer had downloaded on his floppy!
One chap was tearing out his hair, and swearing fit to burst,
So I asked him what the problem was – 'It's Microsoft', he cursed!
I'm trying to put Windows in, and I can't fix all their tricks,
Says I, 'There's boys round Keady put yer windows in with bricks!'

When the thing was ready, no work was left for me,
But to lie in bed in splendour, and watch Kilroy on TV!
The animals had all been trained, for me there was no call,
But I used to wander round at times, to marvel at it all.
The tractor had this guidance thing, worked off a satellite
It could go out totally by itself, to plough, or spread the . . . manure!
It worked all day, from dawn to dusk, and never thought of skiving,
And it never stopped outside the pub, like it did when I was driving!

The pigs, we always reckoned, were as happy as could be,
Rooting round the meadows, in clobber to the knee!
But now they had a toilet, and their own big bathroom suite,
And lived in spotless splendour, with everything so neat.
Their food was all delivered, with plastic forks and spoons,
And they ate with great decorum, in their splendid dining rooms,

A COUNTRY GLIPE

The boar lived in a special pen, with soft romantic lights,
And was visited by all the sows, but only weekday nights.
The computer scheduled him to rest, each Sunday after tea,
And put on Miss Piggy videos on his personal TV.
It checked each sow's contentment scale, after all his sessions,
And a little crushed viagra might be added to his rations!

The gates were opened up each day, sharp at seven am.
And the cows would march, like soldiers, down to the milking pen.
No need to chase them homeward, with whack or casual prod,
And all of them were programmed not to skitter down the road!
Milk production zoomed at once, for each one gave her all,
With her perfect balanced diet, and her soothing milking stall.
And if the vet might have to come, no mess did it entail,
He had a network socket he plugged in beneath each tail!
No need for arms inserted deep, in rectal penetration,
He could see the details all on screen, in graphic presentation!
It would even formulate a cure, with drugs and balms and potions,
For tender tits, or crumpled horns, or thin and greenish motions!
When it came to breeding, there was some queer change in that -
We always used the 'AI Man'- the 'Bull in the Bowler Hat'!
But these cows got on the internet, and God knows what they found,
Great big Blondie Swedish Bulls that were dangling to the ground!
Primrose, Belle and Daisy Mae all took their pick and then,
Ulrika took a fancy to a massive bull called Sven!
Each cow, in turn, picked out her mate, the one she fancied most,
And their love was consummated, and delivered Parcel Post!

The sheep live up the mountainside, in the warmer summer climes,
And I'd send oul' Shep to round them up, to check them out at times.
But none of that oul' whistling stuff, when you wanted him to turn,
You called him on his mobile phone – provided it was on!
The Ram was wearing diamond rings, and a fancy leather jacket,
He said he was a 'businessman' – and making quite a packet!
He had his own wee website, called 'FatAndFluffyLambas',
With pictures of our younger ewes, in 'Baby Doll' pyjamas!
It seems he hired them out to blokes whose love life was not grand,
And invested all the profits in a bank, on the Isle of Man!
A squad went off each weekend to Drumsill and Carrick more,
To wait outside the dancehall, for boys who didn't score!

But of course it ended up in tears, like most good things in life,
For I thought that I would ask them to computerise the wife!
All the parts were working, but some things sagged a bit,
If you seen her in her birthday suit, you might think it didn't fit!
Her engine was still going strong, but the gearbox was away.
She could hardly even climb the stairs, to bring me up my tay!
So they fitted her with microchips, and a wee recharging socket,
And she flew round doing housework, just like a bloody rocket!
She started on them fitness things, till her strength became a menace,
Her legs developed muscles like yon blade that plays the tennis!
She used to lift the sofa up, to hoover down below it,
One day I was lying on it, and she didn't even know it!

And her memory - it was perfect, all recorded on CD,
And then replayed in stereo, to prove how wrong I'd be!
I had to watch each thing I said, even if it made no sense
For every word was taken down, and used in evidence!

Then she got on to the Internet, along with them damn cows,
And learned what she'd been missing – by God there was some rows!
It seemed that other men did things, about which I knew nothing,
Like buying bloody birthday cards, or helping with the shopping!
There's men on there with bodies that looked packed out with rocks,
With teeth like rows of tombstones, and chins like concrete blocks!
And there's other photographs as well, of things I cannot say,
But I caught her staring at the horse, in a longing sort of way!
So life became a torture, from early morn to night,
No matter what I said or did, she knew it wasn't right.
And even in the dark of night, she always wanted more.
It ended up I had to steal that stuff they fed the boar!

There was only the one answer, so I got out the phonebook,
And rung the Ministry Boyo, to get me off the hook.
But he said you've signed along the line, and no way you can gyp,
So I'm going in tomorrow – to get MYSELF a microchip!

The only poem I had left was the one I had been working on since the very first entry, and had been dropped twice, when I got 'better' ideas in between. They used to sing the song 'Bard of Armagh' at the end of the contest, and (not wishing to cause a stampede for the door by singing) I was listening to this, and thinking it would be a lot better story if it was spelled 'BARRED', as in barred from all the pubs in the town! I had added various episodes to the poem over the past few years, some of which are a bit dated now - eg Peter Canavan playing for Tyrone, Johnny Adair and his 'Simply the Best' T-shirts, and Roy Keane's famous Saipan story in the World Cup, with Eamonn Dunphy's unwavering support of him, totally uninfluenced by the fact that he had a book out about him, of course!

As an (almost) 5ft 1inch tee-totaller, getting barred from pubs was not something I was particularly familiar with, so I had to work out a good reason to get turfed out of all the various types of pub found in most towns, and in Northern Ireland, most towns have the IRA pub and the UDA pub, which were the most controversial. Then I was invited to do a night in Armagh Golf Club, which led to one of the best liked episodes in the poem - it was written specially for the occasion.

People often ask me how long it takes to write a poem – most are a few weeks, or even days - but this one took over 4 years!

It was written 'to the tune' of the song, with the first two lines (and the last bit) as similar as possible.

The 'Barred' of Armagh (2005)

Oh, list to the lay of a poor Irish boozer,
And scorn not the groans from his poor withered throat,
For I can't get a drink in my own native city,
And it's really beginning to get on my goat!

I was sitting one night with the lads in my 'local'
When the craic turned to heroes of the great Gaelic game,
McGeeney and Marsden, and others were mentioned,
All known far and wide as men of great fame.
But some bloke from Tyrone chimed in with a mention,
Of a fella called 'Caravan', or something of the kind,
He seemed to think that this bloke was so special,
That the sunshine did emanate from his behind.
The discussion was heated, and remarks became personal,
And parentage sometimes was called into doubt,
And expressions were used that concerned sex and travel,
And numerous insults were bandied about.
Now these things are common with the best of companions,
When football's discussed from the North to the South,
And so in keeping with the finest of Gaelic traditions,
I drew out and hit him a slap in the mouth!
Now you'd think that the barman, being from Armagh city,
Would understand my strong feelings, in this regard,
But the two-faced oul turncoat, he let me down badly,
He roared in my face, "Outside, Boy– You're barred!"

The very next night, I went on a bit farther,
To a pub where soccer was the game that they played,
And fell in straightaway with a great bunch of fellas,
And sure the crack it got better the longer we stayed!
We were SO sorry England were not the World Champions,
But them Boys from Brazil, they were just different class,
And no wonder Roy Keane could not play for Ireland,
With Dunphy's oul' head stuck so far up his ass!
But then I heard one of them footballing arseholes,
Who talk Man United from morning till night,
And never cop on that the rest of the universe,

Thinks that they're just talking absolute . . . Balderdash!
It was 'Giggsy', and 'Keano' and brilliant wee 'Scholesey',
And there's only so much of that crap you can take,
So purely to shut off the dammed noise pollution,
I drew out and hit him a slap in the bake!
Now the barman turned round, and I got a shock,
For across his back of his shirt was wrote 'Beckham'
He refused to accept that I'd the best of intentions,
And he landed me out on the street, so feck'im!

--

Then I thought I would travel a little bit farther,
And the Rugby club bar I would give a look-see,
And sure enough I fell in with a great bunch of fellas,
All built like them wrasslers you'd see on TV.
Now one of the biggest came over, and told me
These boys are all forwards, and men with no fears,
I thought to myself that they looked a bit backward,
For they all had flat noses, and cauliflower ears!
If the forwards were backward, the backs were more forward,
And the three-quarters looked like they'd been in a ruck,
The prop had to lean on the bar to stay upright,
And the fullback was so full that he didn't give a damn!
Now your man tells me this fella here is a hooker,
Indicating a young man exceedingly large,
I'd never met a MAN from that noble profession,
So I thought I would ask him how much did he charge!
This innocent question seemed to greatly annoy him -
Maybe he had not been long in the trade!
But he called me for all the bad names he could think of,
A nasty and noisy abusive tirade!
Now I wanted to hit him a belt on the head,
To show the big bugger how angry I felt,
But I'd have needed to stand on a chair just to reach him,
So I drew up, and gave him the head in the belt!
The barman, he charged round the bar like a rhino,
He refused to accept that it all was a lark,
Grabbed me by the neck and the arse of the trousers,
And landed me half way across the car park!

Well, then I got thinking some more on the subject,
That the bar in the Golf Club might suit to a tee,
I fell in right away with a great bunch of fellas,
The dacentest craythurs you ever would see.
One fella kept saying his wife was a hooker,
But he played with a slice and he couldn't do a thing,
I said not a word, for I'd learned my lesson,
But then sure he asked me what way did I swing!
He asked who I played with first thing in the morning,
A remark I thought personal – it cut like a knife!
He said they were short of a man for a foursome,
Would I like to play a round with him and his wife !
Well, his Missus, she waved across the room at me,
A woman so huge that a bus she could fill,
She'd a grin like a row of headstones in a graveyard,
And a set of false teeth Shergar left in his will!
Well, I thought to myself, this is worse than Ballymena,
As I stood in the corner, with my back to the wall,
Then the wife headed over, and at that point I panicked,
And scattered yer man, as I charged down the hall!

The next night I headed for a part of the city,
Where the kerbs are all painted with gold, white and green,
And all the graffiti was written in Irish,
And there wasn't a tax disc on any windscreen!
I fell in straightaway with great bunch of fellas,
With great big long beards like your man Ronnie Drew
They were talking of setting up a Workers Republic,
Which seemed a bit odd, 'cos they're all on the Broo!
One fellow asked what I thought of Karl Marx
His works, his ideas, his brilliance and flair,
Says I, "The only one I knowed was Groucho,
Was it Karl had the hat, or the wild curly hair?"
He asked me again if I knew much of Lenin,
And the role that he played in the great workers fight,
Says I, "He was great when he worked with McCartney,
But thon Yoko Ono – she wasn't half right!
This fella, he called me an Ignorant Gobshite,
And a Tool of the Capitalist Oppressor to boot.

He shouted "Agus na habair aon focail eile"
As he waggled his finger right under me snout.
Now, sad to relate, I don't speak the language,
What he said was not what I thought I had heard,
So due to the lack of an accurate translation,
I drew out and hit him a smack in the beard!
Now a fella come over and whispered a message,
Says He "Now don't think that I'm trying to be rude,
I reckon you should leave before he recovers,
Unless you've a hankering for Hospital food!"

By now things were bad, so I thought I would venture
To try my luck on the 'far side of the tracks',
So I headed down town, and found a small tavern,
Where all their tattoos had wee Union Jacks!
I fell in with the best bunch of lads you could wish for,
With muscles all bulging out through their vest.
They seemed to be some kind of Tina Turner Fan Club,
They were all wearing T-shirts with 'Simply the best'!
Now the place it was warm, so I took of my jacket,
And the temperature suffered a sudden sharp drop.
But then I copped on at what they were staring,
I'd forgot I was wearing my old Celtic top!
Now they all carried on as if nothing had happened,
A brilliant reaction, if you know what I mean,
Except one wee skitter, who staggered across to me,
Shouting something about what he'd do to Jock Stein!
He described in some detail what he'd do to Our Hero,
In language they should not be teaching in schools,
So to help him control his oul' sexual perversions,
I gave him a bloody good kick in the spools!
As he lay on the floor, sort of groaning and writhing,
The barman wagged me over to have a wee talk,
He says Sammy has friends who are not very friendly
I think you should run, while you're able to walk!

One day I was wandering around up in Thomas Street,
When I spotted a sign saying 'Pub With No Beer',
But I headed in anyway, for by now I was desperate,

A COUNTRY GLIPE

And sat down at the bar, though it looked a bit queer.
The barmaid was older than what I was used to,
And there was only one customer, dressed all in black,
Says I, It's an odd way to run a such a business,
But I'll try a wee whiskey, just for the crack!
Well, she gave me a spiel on the evils of liquor,
She says "This is the Pioneer Temperance Club!"
Says I "Sure Missus, I know what you're meaning –
If it wasn't for drink, I could go down the pub!
Well, your man came across with a tin that he rattled,
We're collecting to save fallen women, says he.
There's no better thing you could do, sure I told him,
If I slip you a tenner, could you save one for me?
The Old Doll, she called me an ungrateful heathen,
A spawn of the Devil, and a black-hearted brute.
Now you surely don't think I would hit an old woman,
So I took a good thump at your man in the suit!
It was not till he fell with his eye sort of blackened,
That I noticed his shirt collar looked a bit queer.
It seems I had walloped a Priest of the Parish,
So I'm bloody well barred from the Pub With No Beer!

Each pub that I enter I get the same greeting,
A rapid Bum's Rush, straight out through the door!
I've had to give up on my wandering and drinking,
For I'm known to each barman as a Nasty Wee Hoor!
So at home with my Kathleen, my poor wife, you'll find me,
Sat by the fire, with a can in my paw,
For there isn't a pub that I dare set my foot in,
And that's why they call me the 'Barred' of Armagh!

I was sent a funny e-mail soon after the 2007 final, which gave me an idea for 2008. It was describing how Noah tried to build the Ark in modern times, and all the building regulations, etc, he would run into, and I really loved the concept. I expanded some of the ideas, took out the more political ones, added a few more, and turned it into yet another 'put-upon farmer' type of poem. It did not win (some fella called Liam McNally arrived, with stories about growing up in Darkest Keady!) but it always goes down well with other audiences round the country.

Noah Hope (2008)

I was dungin' out the calf house, when I got the call from God
He said "Put out that cigarette, and get up, you lazy sod
I've searched this land for 40 days, to find one decent man
But you're all a bunch of sinners, so sod that for a plan
We're going to have another flood – it's that global warming lark.
So for want of a better candidate – I want you to build an ark!"
"Be God, now God", I spluttered, "sure I couldn't drive a nail,
With me in charge, a job like this is surely bound to fail.
Besides, I need to sow the corn, and I've got my spuds to plant,
If I'm getting into building arks, I'm gonna be needing a grant!"
"Don't worry about money" he said with God-like grace,
"We have no accountants here – they're all in the other place"
"I just dropped a load of ready cash in the chest in your back hall"
Says I "I'll shift it to Dundalk, in case the Tax men call!
Well, I had a look at the Bible, just to check up on the plan,
And went off to look for Gopher Wood, 300 cubits long

But they said "endangered species", the man had no idea
He said to go down to Belfast, and look around Ikea!
Well, I got a load delivered, and got started on my labours
Then the damned objection letters came in from all the neighbours!

Well a boyo from the Planners came, on a fact-finding mission,
To see what I was building, and did I have outline permission.
He said I could not build a house, even though it was a boat,
I claimed it was mobile home, because was meant to float,
He quoted regulations till my ears were getting pounded,
I told him there would be a flood, and we would all be drownded
He become quite agitated then, and said "Is that a fact?"
"NO FLOODS till we can study the Environment Impact!"
Then they saw it was a boat, so they called in the DOE
To check the roads for moving it from here to near the sea
They all refused to listen, and they looked at me right queer,
When I tried to explain to them, that the sea was coming HERE!

By now the time was running out, and I didn't know what to do,
So I hired a lock'o'joiners, doing the double on the Buroo.
But now, as an employer, I was caught in far worse hooks
The Equality Commission landed out to check the books.
It seems my workforce profile had to match the local needs,
Two Protestants, two Catholics, and a dozen Portuguese!
We had a couple of Latvians, and a bloke from Senegal
And a pair'o'boys from Derrynoose, who seemed to do feck all!
Then the Union Man arrived – said I was on a sticky wicket.
He said if I got up his nose, then he was going to picket!
The sign we had outside the bogs was difficult to match
It had to be in six languages, including Ulster-Scotch!
I said they'd all pee in the sheugh, it was the easiest solution.
The bloody Rivers Authority were gonna do me for pollution!

Then a nasty letter came, my books I had to render,
A contract of that magnitude, it should have went to tender.
Harland and Wolff insisted that they send a business plan,
And then we got submissions from Korea and Japan.
They all sent fancy brochures, and salesmen came in bunches,
I had to let me trousers out, from all them business lunches
But I just stuck to all my guns, and said the Lord had spoke
I had to build the ship myself, and not just buy some yoke.

Then the Board of Trade turned up, with rules and regulations,
Governing rights of way at sea, and foreign destinations.
I would need to get a GPS, as a guide to a safe haven,
I said I'd just send out a dove, or maybe an old raven
They wanted to see the engines, to check if they burned clean,
And dipped the bloody diesel tank, in case we ran on green!
He looked at my carbon footprint, but I said it did not matter.
The world will not burn that much coal, when it's all under water!
I said we'd run on methane – there'd be no shortage of manure
The boyo gave me a dirty look, and called me a cheeky hoor!
He said we were all amateurs – the insurance man would panic.
I reminded him professionals had built the damn Titanic!
Then we had a visit from the Assets Recovery cops
My bank accounts were frozen like an Eskimo's lollipops
They were asking awkward questions about diesel, fags and drugs
I told them that it came from God – they said "D'ye think we're lugs?"
They need proof of income, printed black and white in ink
I said I saved my milk cheque, and I didn't smoke or drink
Unless I could get proof from God, I was going to be in lumber
So I called in Dr Paisley – He knows God's private number!

A COUNTRY GLIPE

The Vet arrived from the Ministry, to inspect accommodation,
And to check for dung disposal, water, feed and ventilation
I showed him round the cabins, and he said "This just won't do"
"You'll need more room per animal" – I said "This is for the crew!"
Then the food inspectors came, to check all the supplies,
The spuds were just not suitable - they had far too many eyes!
The apples were downgraded, not fit to feed to goats
The corn was too expensive, and I wasn't getting my oats!
The hay was damp and musty, the spaghetti in a tangle
The bananas for the monkeys were all bent at the wrong angle!
The rules and regulations – I didn't know where to begin,
The EEC were very tight on what you could bring in
There'd be no Mad Cows from England, or none with tongues of blue,
No chickens in from Norfolk, in case they had the 'Flu.
I got all of the domestic breeds of horse and sheep and cow,
I didn't bother with the pigs – there's no money in them now
I got crocodiles from Egypt and llamas from Peru,
And I nicked a couple of rhinos from a field at Dublin Zoo

I kept them all in the grazing field, until the time would come,
But I had trouble working out just how the loading should be done
They couldn't march in two by two, in a side-by-side position,
'Cos that would need permission from the Damn Parades Commission!
The badgers had a protest, and swore they'd never yield
Objecting to contentious marches going through their field
The Anti-Hunt protesters were acting quite exultant
They'd called in Brendan McKenna, to act as a consultant!
Then a Orange Order Boyo called and said he wished us well

Just put the elephants in front, and drive them on like hell!

Then God arrived, in splendour, to check how we'd got on,
He said "You haven't got much done – explain yourself, my man!
Well, I told him all the troubles, and why it was so tough
Then he said "The flood is cancelled – I think I've heard enough!
I can stop this Global Warming lark, whose results will be so dire,
I'm going down to Hell right now, to put out the bloody fire!
No point in wasting all that coal, just to make the sinners whine,
The hell yis made here for yourselves is a damn site worse than mine!"
Well, he struck the ark with a thunderbolt, and burned it all to ash,
The animals he disappeared, just like that, in a flash.
I was left with nothing, not a hoof or hair or stalk,
Except a couple of million, in the bank down in Dundalk!
So I'm heading for Las Vegas, a damn good time to find
And it's a long way from the ocean, just in case he'd change his mind!

The firm I had worked with for seventeen years went bust (2 days before payday) in January 2006, and I found myself on the dole for four months. It had come under new ownership several times while I was there, and none of us were greatly surprised that it ended up broke, but the thought of being an unemployed 59-year old computer programmer was not very comforting. However, I did get another job, in Belfast, and I got a poem out of it as well. It is a little exaggerated, but sadly, only a little!

This one has not made it to the Bard finals yet, and probably won't, as I do not think it is good enough, but it helped pass the time while on the Dole, and gave me a little satisfaction too!

Jobseekers Allowance

Now I'm what ye call a stupid oul mug,
For I worked hard all through my life,
To keep the oul wolf away from the door,
For myself and the kids and the wife.
I reaped and I sowed, and I worked on the land,
I shovelled the dung and the soil,
Till my hands were as rough as an oul badger's arse,
From the cold and the heat and the toil.
Then I got a job with computers and such,
And I sat at a desk for my pains,
And I thought to myself that at long and at last,
I had got started using my brains.
But now I have learned how wrong I could be;
The common sense that I have lacked,
For one fine day the receivers walked in,
And told the whole lot we were sacked.
No problem, I thought, I have paid all my tax,
And my stamps and my full contributions,

Sure I'll sign on the dole, and sit on my hole,
And they will make my restitutions!
Well, thought to myself with my stamps and my health,
Sure b'God I just couldn't go wrong.
So I dandered along, and collected a chit,
And sat down with the rest of the throng.
There were lads out of school, in jeans as a rule,
With their knees showing out through the rips,
There were young lassies there, with their bellies all bare,
And wee dolphins tattooed on their hips.
There were accents from all across the wide world,
From Poland, Ukraine, Zimbabwe,
There was even a few of the locals there too -
Lithuanians from near Tandragee
Well, a thing on the wall, my number did call,
With a voice like a computer geek,
And a fella called Graham, just took down my name,
And said to come back Tuesday week!
But, I said, I only come in to sign on,
I got sacked, without my pay packet,
He said there's a queue, so there's nowt we can do,
So there's no point in making a racket.
Well, I filled in a form, forty-six pages long,
And they told me my claim it was sound,
So after a month of running in twice a week,
B'God - I got fifty six pound!
Well, I went in once again, to try to explain,
just why I was getting this strife,
So they said that on my contributions, y'see,
I would get bugger all for the wife.
I explained she'd this habit of eating, y'know,
And she liked the odd Benson & Hedges
When the weather was cold, she insisted on clothes,
to prevent getting blue round the edges
They told me I needed to fill in a form,
to send my claim up for revision,
It was only some forty-six pages long,
I thought I had got double vision.

A COUNTRY GLIPE

The missus would need for to claim income-based,
as she had no stamps of her own,
And we needed to bring in the full evidence,
of every damn thing we did own.
Did I have any money in my bank account;
Credit Union, or 'Save as You Earn'?
Did I have any diamonds hid under the floor,
or a numbered account in Lucerne?
Had I got any cash, in a big offshore stash,
in Euros or maybe gold bullion?
Did I own a van that was used by a man,
Smuggling diesel down by Slieve Gullion?
Well, then they went through all the same for the wife,
Any children we might have concealed?
And the dog and the cats, and the mice and the rats,
And the cow living in the next field
The next bloody question confused me somewhat -
I thought it was fun they were pokin'
They asked if the childer was paying me rent -
Says I, now you've GOTTA be jokin'!
Well, after eight weeks, or maybe some more,
We got put up to eighty-eight pound.
Then some redundancy money came through,
And the feckers, they knocked it back down!

Well, I got me a job, and I'm working again,
But I still feel a bit of a fool,
For now I've caught on just where I went wrong,
All those years ago, when I left school.
For I was a knob, that started a job,
When I quit the schooling, I am thinking,
If I weren't so thick, I'd have signed on the sick,
And started out shagging and drinking,
For if I had ten weans, then the capital gains,
Would keep all my bills in abeyance
I could sit on the dole, just scratching my hole,
and live on the family allowance.
And to go one better, get a wee Doctor's letter,
to say I'm addicted to drink,

For if we're alcoholics - and a total oul bollix,
We would get extra money, I think!
And of course, the best tack, would be have a bad back,
Not that I'd be thinking of skivin'
For I'd get DLA, and an increase in pay,
and a car I could use taxi drivin'!
If I battered the wife, gave her plenty of strife,
the Social would be bending my ear,
With the kids nicking cars, and hanging round bars,
we'd be in Disneyland every year!

The people I met in the buroo office now,
They were all as nice as could be,
But the system it seems, is no longer designed,
To suit oul buck eejits like me
If you spend all your life just learning the rules,
And all of the things you can claim,
If you camp at the office, each day of your life,
Then money will flow down your drain,
But if it is occasional insurance you need,
To help out when you're down on your luck
Then I would suggest highway robbery,
For 'Jobseekers' is not worth a . . . Damn!

I was stuck for ideas for 2009, and fell back on one that I had thought about before – the train journey that I now make every day to and from Belfast, to work. They say that humour is just real life, slightly exaggerated, but this did not even need exaggerating, for all I had to do was re-word the actual events to make them rhyme.

Locomotion (2009)

Standing on the platform, queued up two or three deep,
Just like a crowd of Zombies, all walking in their sleep
Propped up like the living dead, waiting for the train,
Wake up, jump on and grab a seat, and then doze off again!

Thon boyo in the corner there - must be in the building trade,
If he plasters walls like he does his jeans, he'll surely make the grade.
He wears a yellow plastic hat, and a shirt like a lumberjack,
And when the tail of it rides up, you can see right down his . . . underwear!

Then there's a computer geek, with his laptop on the go
He's dressed as if he stole the clothes from a badly made scarecrow
He's plugged in to his ipod, volume turned up to the sky,
His head must just be booming like a Lambeg in July
He's battering at his laptop, with an all-consuming need,
Fingers flying on the keyboard, like an octopus on speed
He's got the latest mobile phone, but he never gets real calls
He just lives his life on Facebook, with his electronic pals
Typing 'Hi, I'm sitting on the train', or to list his latest whim,
Who the hell would give a sh-t, except another geek like him?
He has 'mates' in Albuquerque, Singapore, New York and Rome,
But he hasn't got a girlfriend, and he spends his nights at home.

There's a crowd of kids up the far end, with Ma and Da there too,
Though you might think from all the noise, they were monkeys from the Zoo
Climbing, jumping on the seats, like lunatics on the run
While Mammy sits like a ton of lard, just saying "Stop that, Son"
Screaming 'TRIXIEBELLE HIT MEEEE', and crying them fake tears,
A testament to modern life, and the shortage of thick ears!
There's an Oul Doll sitting just in front, with a woolly hat and glasses,
And steely eye that shows she'd know how to redden a few asses!

Thon lassie in the corner, has the phone glued to her ear,
Bringing her mates all up to speed on the gossip of the year.
It is just like Bloody Hollyoaks, and all shouted down the phone,
With expressions and hand signals, just like she was alone!
Her best friend Kylie got engaged to her dreamboat boyfriend, Wayne,
And then she caught him snogging with her cousin, Mary Jane
And Tyrone is dating Annabelle, but she fancies his mate Gerry,
But he's doing a strong line with a BLOKE from Portaferry!

Then everybody gives a groan, as the train slows to a crawl,
We stop in the middle of nowhere, surrounded by feck all!
The cows are staring from the fields, thinking 'Look - a people truck'
While the passengers stare blankly back, all as bored as . can be
They're having signal problems; there are leaves upon the line,
The snow we had here last weekend was simply the wrong kind

A COUNTRY GLIPE

There's a bomb scare at Kilwilkie, the train in front's broke down,
The Enterprise from Dublin was slow in coming down!
NIR apologise and hope we're in no rush
We all say get it going soon, or we'll get out and bloody push!

You get the same at each evening, hurrying home again
Same people, same old faces, but a bit more cheerful then!
And lots of others there as well, from every land and nation
You see the world and all its works, at Belfast Central Station

---

There's a fella with a bicycle, he takes it on the train,
It is surely grand for keeping fit, but not great in the rain,
His cycling shorts are wringing wet, the padded arse is baggin'
He would probably be drier if he'd swum across the Lagan!
He's dripping like a broken tap, and looks a total prat,
But at least he's guaranteed a space – his puddle sees to that!

There's a bunch of lassies at the station, heading for the city.
Going for a big night out, dressed up to look so pretty.
Clothes like them wee news reports you'd see sometimes on Sky –
Should just cover the essentials, but must catch the viewer's eye!
Skirts that are like pelmets, in keeping with the fashion
Every time they bend a bit, you can see tomorrow's washing!
Wee tops that show their belly, with their bra straps all displayed,
Not cloth enough to tighten up a loose head on a spade!
And they must not have a mirror in their houses at home either,
Some of them have thighs that would shame a Charolais heifer!

Sometimes I'd get the Dublin train - it's called the Enterprise
It does not stop in Lurgan – mind you, that's no surprise!
There's businessmen on mobiles, doing their cross-border tradin'

Then there's oul dolls up for shoppin', 'cos 'da proices is a-mazin!'
There's lots of loud Americans, in clothes you'd never wear.
An explosion in paint shop would be too drab to compare
All seeking their ancestral home – they'd bend your ear for hours
They jest know Grandad was Irish – he was pickled in John Powers!

Some weekends in wintertime, when the Rugby is in town,
You get the Campbell College Chaps, on late train, heading down.
All speaking slightly loudly, in accents fraightfully naice,
All dressed expensive casual, with voices like crushed ice,
Staying for the weekend, in the Gresham, with their pals
To see some rough young gentlemen, play with their odd-shaped balls!

There's people up on guided tours, to see around Belfast
Of all the places in the world, you'd think it would be last!
They've got a bus to run them round the Shankill and the Falls,
And show them all the 'muriels' drawn on the gable walls!
They are huddled in the station foyer, all as nervous as a kitten,
You'd think that if a car backfired, the whole lot would be . . really frightened!

Then there are the readers, who leave all this behind,
And sail away to a different world, purely in their mind.
With Dan Brown or J K Rowling, Robert Ludlum, John Grisham,
Catherine Cookson, Danielle Steele – and that is just the MEN!
There's people reading newspapers, in keeping with their views Some reading the News Letter, and some the Irish News

Their headlines scream in letters black, their tales of shame or glory
You'd never guess to read them, they're reporting the same story!

Thon wee man reading over there, with his nose stuck in a book
He's miles away from all of this – never even takes a look
He'd be on a different Enterprise, far away in outer space,
Or with CSI Miami, on some serial murder case,
He'd never notice what goes on, not a blooming thing he'd see
But there again, you might be wrong – 'cos that wee man is ME!

I read a short story on the Internet a while back, about a scrabble game where all the words came true, and loved the idea. I changed it around a bit, added a few bits, dropped a few bits, and turned it into a poem, which I liked a lot, but it has not made it to the Bard of Armagh yet.

Not Another Word

It's a hot and sweaty summer's day, and I'm sat here with the wife
We've been married forty bloody years, and it's really screwed my life.
Now that I'm retired you see, the whole thing is so much worse.
We see each other all the time, which makes us swear and curse.
I've caught her with the kitchen knife, staring at my back
And several times I've had the urge to wring her bloody neck.
But today is all sweetness and light, a calm between the bitching,
We are sitting playing scrabble, at the table in the kitchen.
The problem is she's winning, and it is bloody hard to take,
As she's crowing like a rooster, with a big worm in its beak!

My letters spelled out MURDER – just what was in my heart,
I put one letter in my mouth, and chewed it as I thought.
I know it's a dirty habit, but it's something I always do
Like a bad sheep farmer – I was fiddling with my 'U'!
An F was lying open, at the far side of the play
I winked, with an optimistic grin, and added 'UCK'!
Don't look at me like that now – I'm not a total clown.
I wiped the slobbers off the 'U', before I put it down

She just glared down at the table, with a disapproving cough,
With an eye that would freeze an iceberg, she just added O.F.F!
I tried to hit her back at once, but my letters were not right
All 'C's, 'K's, and 'X's, without a vowel in sight!

I skipped a turn, and changed them, for I'd no chance in the game,
All I could spell with what I'd got was some Lithuanian's name!
She played 'TOSSER' down the far side, and I replied with 'BITCH'
The look she threw across at me would kill quicks in a ditch!
She played 'KETTLE' down the middle, and she made herself some tea,
Did not so much as ask me if I had a mouth on me

My letters were still awful, so I played the wee word 'FLY'
A bluebottle flew in the window, and went buzzing slowly by.
It dottered round in circles, like an ould boy on the booze.
She played 'SWAT', and knocked its pan in, with a rolled-up Irish News!
I played 'STAB' across the bottom, on a double letter score,
A knife fell off the worktop, and stuck quivering in the floor!
It was getting really spooky, and I did not know what to do
The words that we were playing were starting to come true!
I played 'POISON', staring thoughtfully at her half-full teacup,
But she continued sipping it, and then just drank it up

The game was coming to a close, and I wasn't in contention
I was sweating like a kangaroo at a pickpocket's convention
I was chewing another letter, and I took it out to see
It was not a lot of use to me – I was sucking on my 'P'
'C' 'O' 'K' 'E' was sitting in the rack in front of me,
If I could find a 'H' for 'CHOKE', I might finally be free!
She played 'HATRED' with a nasty look, muttering under her breath,
I thought my chance had come - I used the 'D' to spell out 'DEATH'
I stared across in the useless hope that she might do it then and there
But it didn't work - she added 'WISH', on a double letter square!

A wasp flew in towards her - I put 'STING' down on the board
She used the 'G' for 'GAPSHITE' and never spoke a word!

She got the fifty bonus points, for clearing her last letter
I knew that I had played and lost, her game was so much better!
The damn wasp changed direction, and came at me like a bullet
I jumped back and gasped in horror, and my 'P' shot down my gullet!
I couldn't speak or get a get a breath, I was gasping to get air
I tried to spell out AMBULANCE, as I slid down off my chair,
She sat there, calmly smiling, with a twinkle in her eye,
While she slowly moved the letters, to spell out the word
GOODBYE

After the Queen, (see the 'Winners' chapter) the only way is down, so I thought 'If she is the top of the social ladder, then who would be at the bottom?' And the answer was blazed across the front page of the next day's paper – an X-factor contestant! I rarely watch the show, as the early auditions sometimes look like cruelty to dumb animals, but I still can't escape the headlines about it. It looks like some of the contestants are barely hanging onto the bottom rung of the evolutionary ladder, never mind the social one! So it had to be a 'lady' from West Belfast, with a blonde wig, a big chest (well, even bigger than mine normally is!) and a mini skirt and high heels!

I had taken part in a charity pole-dancing contest a few months before, organised by my daughter, to raise funds for Cystic Fibrosis. I 'danced' (although calling it that would be a flagrant breach of the Trade Descriptions Act) to the Momma Morton song from the musical 'Chicago' – 'If you be good to Momma, Momma'll be good to you', so I already had the outfit.

Yes – when I looked in the mirror, it even scared ME!

The Y factor (2011)

When I seen the Telly advert, I says 'that's the job for me'
They were looking for contestants for X-factor on TV.
Me boyfriend said I hadn't a hope, but then he's a wee bit thick
I think his name is Richard, 'cos his mates all call him Dick!
There was auditions at the Hilton, on the following Tuesday week
And I swore that I would go for it, and not listen to thon geek!

I thought I'd be a sure thing, with me looks and me funky hair
And I used to work in Tesco's, so I must be halfway there!

There wuz other ones from Ulster, like, had made it right'n big
Like Malachi McWot-is-Name, and thon wee lad, E-ogg-han Quigg
And they were all country gapshites – sure I thought it was a pity
They were not cool and sophisticated, not like us'ns from the city!

Well, I wanted for till look me best, so I squeezed out all me zits
Put on me shortest miniskirt, and a wee top to flash me . . . bits
I wore me boots with the six-inch heels – they are genuine black plastic,
But they tighten up me arse a bit, and make me walk fantastic!

I got a taxi down the town, so me makeup wouldn't get messed
The driver tried to touch me up, so he must've been impressed.
He says "Are ye going till a fancy dress, a party for Tarts'n'Vicars?"
I says "Ye durty Oul Brute Ye, get yer oul paws aff me knickers!"

There was a queue right round the Hilton, way out till the BT towers
The wind aff the river wudda skint ye – I wuz standing there for hours
With the toes and heels cut aff me, them boots is not for walking
By the time I got to go on stage, me dogs wuz fairly barking !

A COUNTRY GLIPE

They asked me what I'd like till sing – I said I wud do 'The Rose'
An original by Westlife – What they were laughing at, God Knows!
Well, I done the first verse rightly, but I tried to dance a bit
My heels caught the microphone cord, and I went arse over tit!
My top was stretched to bursting point, and one fell out, by heck!
I wouldn't have minded half as much if I'd washed for a lower neck!

Well, I knew I could depend on Louis – he couldn't have done no better
Sure he would vote for anyone who had owned an Irish setter!
Thon Cheryl blade was different, now – not a nice thing did she say
She was jealous of me looks, ye see – I knowed that right away!
Simon sat with a big long face, and he fiddled with his pen
With he's trousers up round he's oxters, like Ken Dodd's Diddymen
He said that I was awful, like a crow with a frog in its throat,
But I knowed he fancied me like mad, so he gave me a 'YES' vote.

So I got sent away to England, to join up with the strangest bunch
Some of them was definitely a sandwich short of a lunch!
One bloke was very tanned and fit – he ran marathons for fun
He said he was gay, from Liverpool – I'm not surprised he could run!
There was Chinese girl from London, who had a silk split skirt
And a twenty-eight stone Geordie bloke, who never wore a shirt

One fella was in a cowgirl suit, and a pink hat with flashing lights
He said he was a transvestite – he was always stealing my tights!

There was a funny looking lassie, with blonde pigtails tied to her cap
She said she come from Iceland – I thought she worked in the shop!
Some of them were just hopeless – not one interesting thing.
One fat oul doll from Scotland, sure all she could do was sing!

Of course, the newspapermen went mad, to get all me details
Hunting for some scandalous things to boost their bloomin' sales
The Mirror and the Sun sent men, the Sunday World and the Daily Star
They were camped outside me mammy's like an army going to war.
The bloke from the Protestant Telegraph now - he got a nasty shock
Him and the Andytown News man had been in the same H-block
Then they heard a rumour – now God knows from where it sprung
Me Aunt Bridie had been a hooker, way back when she was young
But they got the details wrong, of course, as these guys usually will
Before she'd the operation, he used to play at Ravenhill!

Me boyfriend sold his story till some newspaper tycoon
He said that we were so in love, we'd be married when I won
G'way'n' ketch yerself on, son!! - if I should win the crown,
There's a damn sight livelier men than him lying in Milltown!

When I sitting with me showbiz pals, chatting to Ant and Dec,
D'ye think I'd want thon spotty twerp hanging round me neck?

The madness just continued, each day crazier than the last
We got to meet the rich and famous, that you'd never see in Belfast
They brought in Jedward just to show it's all right to be crap
But I couldn't get quite close enough to hit one of them a slap
But I only lasted the first three weeks, for they fixed the bloody vote
The tricks them crafty English pull, it would really get on yer goat
They fixed the damn computers – only one vote each could be used
Sure all my fans in West Belfast were totally confused!

Well, I didn't care who won it then, I didn't even switch it on
Some skinny bitch with implants and a voice like a damn foghorn.
But I'm telling yis now – this time next year, I'll have my share of fame
For Mary Immaculata McGonnigle is gonna be a really BIG name!

Another one that was written while I was on the dole, and was not funny enough to make the Finals, was based on a famous poem that Da used to recite - 'The Shooting of Dan McGrew', by Robert Service.

It is a tale of the Klondike Gold Rush of the 1890s - Dangerous Dan is sitting with his 'light of love, the lady that's known as Lou' in the saloon, when a stranger staggers in from the freezing Arctic night. He plays a terrible, sad tune on the saloon piano, and then pulls a gun, and he and Dan blaze away at each other, as the lights go out. When the light comes back on, both are dead, but 'the lady that's known as Lou' is with the stranger, (stealing his poke of gold dust) rather than with Dan, hinting at the possible reason for the gunfight.

I moved this terrible tale to Portadown, and made Dan a Buckfast Delivery man!

Seventy percent of all the Buckfast Tonic Wine sold in N. Ireland is reputed to be drunk in the Portadown/Lurgan area, and it is possible to ring up certain Taxi firms, and get a bottle delivered to your door - wrapped in a brown paper bag, of course, as discretion is all part of the service! In fact, even the door is not necessary - your squat, or your current location in the park or the old tow-path under the bridge at the River Bann will do equally well, provided cash is rendered on delivery!

I re-wrote this one, adding more insults, for the 2012 Bard finals.

Dangerous Dan McHugh (2012)

A bunch of the boys were whooping it up,
in a Portadown saloon,
Some kid was feeding the jukebox,
to put on an Emimem tune.
The smokers were all standing out on the street,
trying to stay out of bother,
And a wheen'o'young drunks in band uniforms
were kicking the dung out of other!

Now down by the band, with a pint in his hand,
sat Dangerous Dan McHugh
And sat by his side, was his blushing bride,
Big Patricia that works in the 'broo.
Well, I'm telling Yis now, she was one ugly cow,
with a face that would scare Simon Cowell
Lipstick and mascara, wheeled in by the barra,
and slapped on with a plastering trowel
Her bra, it was said, was size 84Z,
with reinforced steel in the hook
She was twenty-five stone of muscle and bone,
with more chins than a Chinese phone book

Now Dangerous Dan was a skinny wee man,
But his feet were just damnably smelly
And his legs were that bowed, that everyone knowed,
He could never cap a pig in an alley

He wore great big glasses, like beer-bottle asses
So he looked like a Volkswagen dashboard
He was quite highly strung, 'cos when he was young,
His Ma used his ribs for a washboard.
He'd a look on his mug, like a broke Toby Jug,
And his nose had a drip that hung downwards,
In fact if our dog, had such an ugly phizog,
we'd shave his arse and make him walk backwards

For if you are stuck, or just down on your luck,
　　He'd be the first number you'd tag,
　He'd arrive at full throttle, and deliver a bottle,
　　of Buckfast, in a brown paper bag!
　He was known from Drumcree, out to Tandragee,
　　and from Lurgan to Killycomaine,
And by the Bann bank, where the skinheads all .... drink,
　　they'd erected a shrine to his name
　But Dan was a man, who would deal cash in hand,
　　no drink till you coughed up the wonga
　He'd a big hurley stick, which he use bloody quick,
　　And your knees wouldn't work any longa!

　It was coming half nine, and was all going fine,
　　When the door was slammed open right back
　And a man staggered in, smelling strongly of gin,
　　looking rougher than oul' Father Jack!
　But Dan he turned pale, and his heart it did quail,
　　for he knew that the stranger meant trouble,
And beneath her mascara, Big Patricia looked 'tarra',
　　and her chins all started to wobble!

　He'd an oul overcoat, buttoned up to his throat,
　　and a dung graip was hung from his belt
　He says "Boys, I have come, for to kill a wee scum,
　　and to bury this graip in his pelt.
　For I was the man, who invented the plan,
　　for delivering the bottles of Bucky
　And Big Patricia and me, lived the life of Riley,
　　in a mobile up near Knocknamuckley

He shouted "Now Dan, you are going down the pan,
　　for I'm hauling you over the coals,
You'll be needing some tape, for I'm taking this graip,
　　and making you four new arseholes
　For when I am done, you'll be houlin' your bum,
　　you will not be looking so cute,
　You dirty oul dog, you'll going to the bog,
　　like an Orangeman playing the flute"

A COUNTRY GLIPE

Well, Dan, he jumped up, spilling half of his cup,
and roared "Patricia, This thing is a farce"
"Hand me that hurley stick", which she did double quick –
it was hid down the sheugh of her arse.
Well, the fight might have gone right through to the dawn,
But the end quite suddenly come
When Dan's final cut, hit yer man on the nut
He was split like a bricklayer's bum!
And Dan too was going; his wine had quit flowing,
with the graip buried deep in his hide,
It stuck six inches in; he was that bloody thin,
it was three inches out the far side.
He lay gasping his last, and lamenting his past,
for at last he had started to think,
For that now he was bate, he had found out too late
you should never mix weemin and drink!

10 POEMS : THE WINNERS!

I had a poem almost done for 2004, but the firm I worked for went out for Christmas Dinner at the end of 2003 - to a Chinese Restaurant. I really enjoyed the meal, but the thought struck me as incongruous, and became by far my best poem to date. They say the best poetry comes from the heart, but this one came from the stomach!

It tells the tale of an elderly farmer, unused to modern eating establishments, and the sad effects of modern culinary diversity on a well-matured Irish Agricultural digestive system. This one always seems to strike a chord with audiences all over the country, especially the vindaloo story, which many of them seem to have experienced!

I never touch the stuff myself, of course . . .

Foreign Feedin' (2004 Winner)

Now you might say I'm a Country Glipe, and you wudn't be far wrong,
For I was reared on spuds and tay, and the tay was right and strong!
There was porridge for the breakfast and soda bread for supper,
And all the spuds that you could eat, with great big lumps of butter!
Now I've wheen 'o' youngsters, and they've all growed up right grand,
But they take me out till places that I just can't understand.
They'd land round on a Sunday, and lift me and the wife,
And head off till atein' houses that I'd never seen in my life!

We went till this Italian place, done up in golds and reds,
A big long name with letters that were mostly A's and Z's!
The waiter hovered round me, muttering 'pizza this and that',
So I pointed a something, and says 'I'll try a piece o' that"
Well, he landed with a plate of stuff, the size of a manhole cover.
It looked just like a pancake that someone had boked over!
Says I, 'Is this recycled?', for bejapers I'd have swore
That it looked as though it had been ate at least the once before!
Well, I tried me best till cut it, but it stuck together like glue,
There was cheese all down my trousers, and tomatoes on my shoe.
I didn't get the half of it, although I tried me very best,
It was just like sucking chewing gum from out of a string vest
---
Then one week we went Chinese, which caused a puzzled frown.
For the menu had wee pictures, and was written up and down!
I pointed at this item that looked like a Christmas tree
And a thingy with a leg stuck up, like a wee dog having a pee.

The waiter brought a bowl of stuff that looked like thinnish mud,
With lumps of stuff that floated – I don't think it was a spud!
He says 'That there is bird's nest soup – it is really quite refined',
Well, it tasted like the bird had flown, but had left a lot behind!
Then we got big bowls of rice, with lovely lumps of pork,
But they gave us a couple of bits o' sticks, instead of a knife and fork!
I was rummaging about with these, chasing this and that,
But half of it landed down my shirt, and the rest was on the mat!

Then we tried the Mexicans, with peppers green and red,
And things they called tortillas that looked like pirta bread,
They had tacos and burritos, enchiladas and all that,
And stuff that they called chilli, but bejapers, it was HOT!
We had sauerkraut, and schnitzel, risotto and kebabs,
And some of that Italian bread, that looks like concrete slabs.
We tried every bloody restaurant, and every flaming dish,
We even tried that sushi, but it tasted just like fish!

One week we tried an Irish Place, with 'traditional' décor!
They'd a bike nailed to the ceiling, and a pishpot by the door!
I looked in vain for spuds and steak, but such food was lacking drama
It was "honey-roast medallions of corn-fed Peruvian llama"
They had potato wedges – they would NEVER call them chips,
All with multi-coloured salads and guacamole dips!
I asked about some sausages, and maybe a bowl o' champ,
The durty look they gave me, you'd have thought I was a tramp!

Then we tried a new French place, called the 'A La Carte'
The waiters all looked down their nose, as though you'd let a fart!
They handed me this menu, which was a crying shame,

For the only bit that I could read was the bloody printer's name!
The writing was all fancy, with long curlicues and stuff,
But there was one word I recognised, amongst all that foreign guff.
L'Escargot -- was a racehorse, that run in the Grand National,
Though till ate him after all these years might seem a bit irrational!
Begob, when He was at himself, he was bloody hard till bate,
He might kinda stringy now, but you'd know what's on yer plate!
Well, it seems that my deduction was somewhat was off the rails.
When the waiter brought my order, sure it was a plate of snails!
Now I says to them 'That's bird food, - I'll not beat about the bush'
What the hell d'yis take me for – d'yis think I'm a bloody thrush?
Well, it turns out that they breed them, on special farms, by heck!
How the hell would you get a grip, when you went to wring their neck!
Now it's far from me to pass remarks on others' atein' habits,
But one thing in their favour – they'd be easier caught than rabbits!

But the final straw was the Indian place, called the Star of Old Bengal,
The waiter's head was bandaged up – he must have had a fall.
We had this stuff called vindaloo – looked like liquid yellow man,
I dunno where the 'VIN' came from, but the 'LOO', I understand!
Well, I started for till ate it, and the sweat began to pour.
It was running down the sheugh o' me arse, and dripping on the floor!

Well, I opened up me collar, and I threw me coat away,
But I was steaming like a dunghill, opened on a frosty day.
We were all back in the motor, heading out for home,
When I noticed things was not quite right, in the nether region zone.
Well, me belt began to tighten, and me face began to frown,
For I could feel things start to loosen, a wee bit lower down!
I was sitting there with buttocks clenched, shouting 'faster faster',
For the pressure gauge was in the red, and coming near disaster!
The car had not stopped rolling, when I burst out of the back,
And hit the door like the Drug Squad, raiding a house for 'crack'
There was buttons flying right and left, as I charged along the hall,
If I'd been a second slower, I'd have pebble-dashed the wall!
The wife came banging on the door, roaring off her head,
But I shouted 'Jasus, Woman, it's coming out like thread!'
I've been sitting waiting for a break, for over half an hour,
I've got a hump across my back like a wee calf with the scour!
You'd need to get me a bloody cork, if you really need to go,
But she says, 'I've used it for myself – I've already filled the po!'

Well, I swore an oath upon that bog, as I sat in pain and rage,
To live on spuds and butter, till I died of great old age.
If I should win the lottery, revenge was on my mind,
I'll buy a place in India, and pay them back in kind.
I'll open an Armagh restaurant, and feed them spuds and sodas,
And lots of greasy sausages, till tighten up the buggers!
Chronic constipation will follow in my train,
For if they were reared on vindaloo, they'll never dung again!

I did not have anything in mind for the following year, so I fell back on an idea I had been kicking around for a long time. I've always known a bit about country music, and laughed at some of the fantastic song titles, and the propensity for disaster that seems to rule the lives of the writers! I found a website with the 'Best Worst Country Songs' - wonderful stuff like "Don't stand out in the wheat field, Maggie, you're going against the grain", "Drop kick me, Jesus, through the goalposts of life", and my personal favourite, "I'd sooner pass a kidney stone than another night with you".

It was a short step to join these up with an Irish Showband theme, and the CullyBackey Cowboy was born. I always say I hold no particular animosity towards Cullybackey - it happens to be a word of the right length, beginning with 'C', and everyone knows that all the cowboys in Coalisland are in the building trade! This poem has a couple of dozen country song titles hidden in the words, and anyone who gets them all wins a free night out in Loughgall - a lovely wee place to live, but it has one shop, and no pubs.

Excitement dies down fairly quickly on early closing day!

The Cullybackey Cowboy (2006 Winner)

Now I'm what you'd call a Rhinestone Cowboy,
I'm a Country Boy through and through,
From my 10-gallon hat to the dung on my wellies,
And the grass that I smoke must be blue!
I can eat beans and bacon, and fart with the best,
I can spit wads of chawin' tobaccy,
I am just like John Wayne, but for one minor pain –
I was born and reared near Cullybackey.

M'Da was a drummer in a Rock'n'Roll Band
My Ma loved all things that were Yank,
I was born one morning, when the sun didn't shine,
They upped and they christened me Hank.
At four in the morning, when I started bawling,
And could not be persuaded to snooze,
My Maw would put whisky into my bottle -
I was brought up on Rhythm'n'Booze.
I took to the singing, before I learned talking,
Anything from Country to Rock.
We all learned to sing pretty loud in our house –
The bathroom door had no lock.
But this Country Music is not all plain sailing,
It brought nothing but trouble and strife,
For all of my songs have begun to come true,
And it really has screwed up my life.

The Gal that I married was called Peggy Sue
From a village in the County Tyrone,
Her Paw was a rancher, with two hundred Friesians
On green green grass of home.
Their cows won the medals at the big County Show,
Their milk always got the top bounty,
And her Paw, he was known from the Moy to Strabane,
As the "Cow-Herd of the County"
We would always meet up at the carnival tent,
Situated some way out of town,
And she would be waiting, down by the riverside,

A COUNTRY GLIPE

With a blanket laid out on the ground.
Well, the story turned out, just like it was Dallas,
Our misdeeds they soon started telling,
For though I am no oilman, I've been known as JR,
And pretty soon, she was Su-wellin'!!
Her Paw and her brothers came calling around,
They said they did not want a quarrel
But the wedding invitation that they handed to me
Was tied to a big shotgun barrel!
She wanted a honeymoon in the Wild West
To see Cowboys and Injuns get shot.
All I could afford was a week in Bundoran,
And that's about as wild as it got.
We got bed and breakfast in this old house,
In a room with a great big green door.
I thought I was picking up good vibrations,
It was the landlady banging the floor

Now Peggy Sue claimed she was eating for two,
And she simply could not get her fill,
From the old candy store on the corner,
Or the Macdonald's up on the hill.
She grew and grew till she blocked out the sun,
As the birth of our child neared its onset,
Her flannelette drawers hung up on the line,
Looked just like red sails in the sunset.
I worked for a while with her Da on the farm,
He used to call me the grim reaper.
I asked why his cows were all black and white,
He told me the licence was cheaper.
He was always yappin' and whingin' at me,
Till I told him it just had to stop
He went on so I chucked him, right into the slurry -
Sort of 'slurry with a whinge on top'!

Well, I tried to improve my Cowboying skills,
At a riding school out near the Moy,
But my four-legged friend was an evil big brute,
With a real nasty look in his eye.

He put his left leg in, and his right leg out,
And he did a great big Hucklebuck,
And I flew like an eagle right over his head
And landed full slap in the sheugh,
As I lay in the drain, in considerable pain,
With my bruises all growing bigger,
I never did find out that oul' horse's name,
But what I called him sounded like Trigger!
Well my saddle sores worsened, and became haemorrhoids,
Bejapers, the pain it was dire,
So I went to the Doctor, and tried to explain,
That I just had a pure Ring of Fire
He said Gentian Violet is the thing that you need,
So I had to call in Peggy Sue,
And I cried out each dawn, as she painted it on,
Singing Don't it make your brown eye blue!

I got my own showband, and we went on the road,
If Hugo Duncan is cool -- we were colder!
We appealed to the more mature kind of fans,
Like Daniel O'Donnell's, but older.
The grannies went wild everywhere we performed,
When I went up on stage with the lads.
Our groupies would gather all along the front row,
And throw up their incontinence pads.
A mob of them gathered outside the hall,
Kicking the doors down to find us.
We broke out and ran like hell for the van,
With the Zimmer frames rattling behind us!

Of course I was tempted by the sex and the drugs,
And the lifestyle was making me sick.
All the travelling in vans and the smoky oul' bars -
I was main-lining aspirins and vick,
The older the fiddle, the sweeter the tune,
The oul dolls would say, with a squeeze,
When they took off their vest, and sometimes the rest,
There were bits hanging down to their knees!

A COUNTRY GLIPE

Well, of course, Peggy Sue was not too well pleased,
With the lifestyle that I was now leading
She decided to follow a different showband,
In spite of my begging and pleading.
She travelled the country in an oul camper van,
Following your man Dickie Rock.
When I asked her the reason, she said with a grin,
That he had a much bigger. . record collection!

Well, by now I was well down the slippery slope,
So I thought that I must bite the bullet.
They said the Mayo Clinic is where all the stars go,
So I took a weekend in Belmullet.
I just went 'cold turkey' to clear out the drugs,
I ate nothing else for a week.
I was that constipated I drunk Syrup of Figs,
Damn near blew a hole in my cheek!

So I'm making a comeback -- I've got a new band
I think we'll go down like a bomb
All of our songs sound exactly the same
Well, it worked pretty well for Big Tom!
Hugo Duncan and me are gonna do a duet,
He says that we can be the best,
For he's the boy to put the 'ree' into 'countree'
And he reckons I can put in the rest!

I had another poem done for the next year's entry, but then I came across a funny article about the differences between men and women, and got the notion of turning my favourite farmer into something completely different! It mentioned things like 'Men can pile an infinite amount of dishes in the sink, without ever noticing that they need washed' or 'Women can remember the price of every item in the house, and who gave them every wedding present, even after forty years'. 'Women can remember every outfit they wore at every event in their entire lives, but men can hardly remember what they wore yesterday, unless it is still lying in the heap on the bedroom floor'. These stereotypes are breaking down a little nowadays, with 'nineties men' who are 'getting in touch with their feminine side', and 'understanding' their wives, etc.

If you saw a bunch of men talking in my young day, the subject was invariably football, hunting, or the price of cattle. Anything else would have been unthinkably effeminate. A group of young blokes talking earnestly together these days might well be swapping recipes for goulash!

BUT - not farmers! Most of them wouldn't recognise their 'feminine side' if it jumped out and hit them with its handbag, so this poem worked all the better for being so incongruous. I borrowed a woman's hat from my daughter for the Bard Finals night, and changed my usual badly battered cap for it, just before the 'Daniel O'Donnell show' part, which went down a treat. Even the judges noticed that I enjoyed 'being a girl' rather more than a man of my advanced years and numerous grandchildren ought to!

HRT (2007 Winner)

I'm a farmer, at that certain age, when things begin to go,
Like waist and hair, and things down there, that kinda thing, you know?
The wife is on thon HRT, and lots of pills and potions,
And is getting fancy hairdos, and lots of funny notions.
Well, her and me, had words, ye see - one thing led to another,
And begod she upped and left me, and run off with another!
Well, I himm'd and ha'd a day or two, and thought she would be back,
But after about a fortnight, my resolve began to crack.
I was getting tired of bread and jam, and needed a good roast,
If I only knowed the recipe, I'd have tried to make some toast!
The fridge was totally empty; there was nothing on the shelf
I was ateing beans from the saucepan, 'cos I'd used up all the delft!
Well, one night I got to thinking, that my life is worth damn all,
So I found a great big bottle of pills, and resolved to end it all.
I got a mug of water, and put the bottle to my head,
And I horsed the whole lot intae me, and headed aff to bed.

Well, I woke up feeling brilliant, and I couldn't tell the reason,
I knew at once I wasn't dead, because my feet were bloody freezing!
I found the empty bottle of pills, and got my glasses out to see,
And realized I'd swallowed three months supply of HRT!
I washed and shaved, and changed my shirt, and felt like a new man,
Then I headed for the kitchen, to hunt out the frying pan.

Well the sink was piled with dishes, and it gave me such a fright
How the Hell had I not seen that, when I went to bed last night?
The cooker top was minging, and the floor was black with grime,
So I started in to cleaning up, and I just forgot the time.
There was not one thing in that whole house that didn't get a wash.
I was oxter deep in Ajax, Cillit Bang and Vim and Flash
I used up all the Fairy Liquid, and begod, it never fails
It even lifted the cow dung from underneath my nails!
I dusted all the ornaments, and the presents from the past
But I could tell you when each one was bought, and exactly what it cost!
I collected all the washing - it was piled up to the sky
And I separated out the whites, though I had no idea why,
I stared at the knobs on the washing machine, in total bafflement,
And realized to my surprise, that I knew what some of them meant!
Well, I got it up and going, and then I made myself some tay,
And I rung Oul Mrs McGoldrick, just to see what she had to say.
I totally surprised myself, at some of the things I said,
Her daughter had a new baby, and I asked how much it weighed!

Well, I headed out round dinnertime, to clean up the pigsties,
Pausing just to change my wellies, 'cos they didn't match my eyes!
I changed my routine slightly, I'm not sure exactly how,
But I got this urge to warm my hands, before I milked the cow.
I wore my brand new dungarees, tucked into my wellie tops,
But every couple of minutes, I kept adjusting the straps!
I felt so full of energy, that I just could not sit still,
I was washing, hosing, painting, and scrubbing with a will.

Before the week was out, Begod, You wouldn'ta known the place,
Everything so shining bright, it could be seen from outer space!
I tried to lie and watch TV, and scratch my nether regions,
But I just kept seeing things to clean – ideas came in legions.
I sat through Coronation Street - thon Norris gets my goat
And I even watched the adverts, without flicking the remote!
I moved round all the furniture, I washed and cleaned the beds,
I re-shuffled the machinery, outside in all the sheds,
I couldn't start the silage, for I didn't want to be seen
With a big RED silage trailer, when the bloody tractor's GREEN!

So I thought I'd take a mini break, just for a couple of days,
To see if I could settle down, and cure this cleaning craze.
So I hunted out my suit and cap, and gave the welly boots a wipe,
And headed off to Keady, with the tractor full'o'the pipe!
I went in to one of them hair saloons, to tidy up the thatch,
The chairs were all black leather, and the 'boys' all dressed to match
The one that done it seemed surprised, for he asked me at least twice,
But I got a very nice blue rinse, and he only charged half price!
The next day was a Thursday, and I thought that I just might go,
And take the train down to Balmoral, to see the Agricultural Show,
Well, I headed off right early, but just as the train was stopping,
I got this sudden awful urge – I NEEDED to go SHOPPING!
I just could not control myself, so I had to sit back down,
And got off at Great Victoria St, and headed down the town!

The sale was on at Debenhams, and so I simply had to stop,
Some things cost only TWICE as much as they would in a

normal shop.
They had all these great designer clothes, laid out on this big table.
Twenty quid for a pair of jeans, plus fifty for the label.
I must have spent an hour or two, in women's underwear,
I was strangely drawn to garments that I knew I couldn't wear
I got a lot of funny looks from all them city slickers,
Feeling all the brassieres, and stretching all the knickers,
I wandered round soft furnishings, with great deliberating
Their range of scatter cushions was quite simply fascinating
I bought a mat for beside the fire, to cover a wee burnt patch,
Then I had to get new curtains, because the old ones didn't match.
And then I saw a three-piece suite, that would suit them all so nice,
And I saved a ball of money, 'cos the mat was just half price!
I headed for the shoe shop, 'cos I hadn't a thing to wear,
It took the most of the afternoon to choose the right five pair.
I got myself a couple of suits, 'cos mine was not that great
I had got it from a bomb-damage, in nineteen seventy-eight
I got myself a wardrobe – a flat pack from MFI,
The last one I attempted was enough to make you cry.
It leaned a kinda sideways, and I could not get in the rails
It ended up I fixed it with a wheen of three inch nails
But this time it was easy, it did not break my heart
I just read the instructions, before I made a start!

I went to a Daniel O'Donnell show, and met this strange big woman,
She's got her own wee farm as well, so we have a lot in common
Her hair's a blue rinse crew cut, and she wears big dungarees,
And a pair of them Doc Marten boots, laced right up to her knees.
I was wearing my pink boiler suit, and she kinda dandered over,
And asked me round to her place, to help fix her front end

A COUNTRY GLIPE

loader
She thinks the oul' hydraulics gone, for she can't get it to rise,
But when I get out my tool kit, she might get a big surprise!
So you never know what lies ahead, what the next event will be,
For life's just one big adventure, for a bloke on HRT!

I was thinking of various ideas for 2010 - Scrabble being the main one, but I was watching the news on TV one night, when a Royal visit to somewhere came on. The Queen was smiling nicely, being introduced to dozens of fat so-and-sos in pin-striped suits, shaking hands, smiling at them all, looking so terribly interested in what ever rubbish they were waffling about. Phillip was walking behind, hands behind him as usual, looking even more interested in the whole thing, and I thought to myself, "Mrs Windsor, I wouldn't want your job for all the diamonds in your tiara!"

And then I thought of a way to make it more interesting. . . .

I spotted a cream hat and pale blue coat in a charity shop for a fiver, that looked appropriate - a friend sent me a picture of the Queen wearing an almost identical outfit in the paper a few months later! I cut up an old grey wig, and stuck it around the edges of the hat, and got a nice little handbag to complete the ensemble, and it went down a treat, especially as there was huge publicity about her visit to Ireland at that time.

Her Majesty's Pleasure (2010 Winner)

One is sure you recognise One – you'll have seen One on TV
Opening things, and closing things, and waving quite nicely
One's been Queen for simply ages – One's Diamond Jubilee is due
But to tell the truth, One's bored to death with all the ballyhoo
Flying here, and driving there, at each ones beck and call
Greeting boring arseholes in just every port of call
Businessmen and councillors, and rogues who are on the make!
One would need to count one's fingers after each handshake!
Opening schools and hospitals, planting trees and being 'nice'
The tabloids think that One is broke, if One wears the same hat twice!

Those Palace Garden Parties – thousands in for tea and grub
Stealing cuttings off the plants, and peeing behind a shrub
Big Fat Boring Bishops, dressed up like a silly twit
Binmen getting MBEs, for a lifetime shovelling . . . rubbish
The Royal Variety performance – One does not like to bitch
But most of them are only on TV to make Simon Cowell rich

One's children are no comfort – they cause One endless strife
The eldest talks to vegetables - which may explain his wife!
The second one got married to that loud, red-headed girl
And the youngest is an actor – as far as One can tell.

All those awful trips abroad – the strange things one sees and hears
Yet another jolly tribal dance – huge painted chaps with spears
Young girls with all their wobbly bits bouncing in a ring
One has to watch One's husband – he likes that kind of thing!
Mind you, the English are the worst, upon every village green
If One sees another Morris Dance, One thinks that One will

scream
Those walkabouts in Africa, in the burning midday sun
The sweat is clinging to One's back, and running down One's bum!
The endless foreign banquets – strange foods to make One choke
If One sees another baked sheep's eye, One feels like One will boke!
And those awful foreign Diplomats – some have simply got no class
That bounder Berlusconi actually tried to grope One's ass!

The opening day of Parliament – Do we really need it?
You think that speech is boring – One has to blooming READ it!
Black Rod walks right in front of One, in tight trousers of black satin
An 'ANUS horriblis' – and One is not speaking Latin!
Of course it used to be much worse – One hates to make a scene,
But that dreadful Thatcher person- she thought that SHE was Queen!
And Blair – forever grinning! Wilson, Heath and Douglas Hogg
One even knew Old Churchill – the real one – not that dog!

Of course One has One's horses – One likes a good hard ride
A thoroughbred between one's legs is constant source of pride
One rides a sensible old mare, who would not do something silly
But One's Husband likes a canter on a friskier young filly!
One's little dogs are fun, of course – they try to bite the staff
Too short to reach the footman's bum, but it does give One a laugh!
The Corgis come from Wales, of course – it might be because of that
That they do things on the carpet, and try to shag the cat!

A COUNTRY GLIPE

One asked one's husband how he copes – tall chap? Phil the Greek!
He shouted 'Dammit Woman, is your brain completely weak?
You should get yourself half plastered before you start the day,
And keep some in your handbag, to make sure you stay that way!
The Old Queen Mum, she knew the way to keep that happy grin
No wonder she kept smiling – she was full of bloody gin!
Could you not smell the blasted stuff - the pong was hard to miss?
She was over ninety years of age – One thought the smell was piss!

So One thought One might try his advice – follow it to the letter
And being Queen is FUN again – One's life is SO much better,
One just has a couple of stiff ones, before One starts the day
And re-fuels from One's Handbag, at the stops along the way.
One nips off to the toilet, and swallows a quick gin
It has all been freshly painted, so no one can smell a thing!

Of course, One tries to match the drink to what One does that day
Create some interest in the job, I suppose, as One might say
If One should be in France, perhaps, a Beaujolais Neuveau
Or if One is going to Scotland – a wee Bell's, 'Afore Ye Go'
And if One is going to Lurgan – One should be so unlucky
One's maid can have a paper bag, containing a bottle of Bucky!

So being Queen is fun again – One greets each day anew,
One sees life through a pleasant haze, thanks to the Devil's Brew
Those chaps seem much less boring, and their chat seems erudite

One no longer gives a toss if they talking total . . . balderdash
But One must be very careful, anytime One has to speak
One's husband drops a clanger almost every other week!
They say that he's a racist, but he is really not one bit
He hates everybody equally, and he does not give a . . damn.

Still, now and then, One gets the urge to loosen up the hold
Do something really different, just to break the mould!
There's an EU banquet on tonight – everyone dressed up so swank
With that big wide German woman, who looks like a Tiger tank
The tiny Frenchman with his wife - another new designer dress!
And that big fat ugly Irish chap - who always looks a mess
One might need a little extra booze, to survive that kind of scrum
So if Old Berlusconi's there, One might just grab HIS bum!

ABOUT THE AUTHOR

Jimmy Rafferty was born and bred exactly as described in this book!

He worked as a 'hoer' (hoeing the weeds, of course!) in the Ministry of Agriculture Research Station in Loughgall for several years, (where he met his future wife, Christina Hughes) before going to the West of Scotland Agricultural College in Ayr. He had jobs in Wales and Scotland before moving back to N.Ireland in 1976, to work in the Goodyear factory in Craigavon.

When Goodyear closed down in 1983, Jimmy went back to school at Portadown Tech, and the Open University, to re-train as a computer programmer. He worked in Lurgan (Expert Information Systems) for seventeen years, programming car insurance, while teaching part time at the Tech in the evenings. When the firm closed in 2006, he worked as a programmer at Allstate N.I., in central Belfast, for seven years, before retiring, aged sixty-six, in 2013.

Jimmy and Tina have three children – Anne, born in Wales, Deirdre, born in Scotland, and Michael, born in N.Ireland - and they have ten grandchildren.

He has always been a great reader, trying anything from Dennis Wheatley to Catherine Cookson, with a lot of science fiction, (Heinlein, Asimov, Doc Smith) westerns, (Lamour, Tuttle) crime thrillers (Deaver, Connolly, Patterson) and above all, comedy (Wodehouse, Pratchett, Sharpe) He tried his hand at writing 'funny poems' for the Goodyear Union newsletter, and then more comedy while at Expert in Lurgan. He first took part in the 'Bard of Armagh' contest in 2001, and has been there every year since, winning four times. This is a contest for 'humorous verse', held every year in Armagh City Hotel, in front of a audience of over a thousand people, with a tremendous atmosphere. Tickets are sold out every year, and would still be sold out if the hall was twice the size! It has become a major attraction in the city, drawing aspiring poets from as far afield as England, Australia, the USA, and Keady!

Most of the poems in this book are available on CD – just visit the website for details .
http://www.jimmyrafferty.co.uk

For information an the Bard of Armagh contest, see
http://www.bardofarmagh.com

Jimmy on You Tube >>
http://www.youtube.com/watch?v=nAJyljj2q6k
http://www.youtube.com/watch?v=ycmm_6R7ISg
http://www.youtube.com/watch?v=aPpDNVZIusY
http://www.youtube.com/watch?v=8ZbniXKmTlk
http://www.youtube.com/watch?v=ppcTo2Eh2Vg